A story that's been brewing for 300 years

SHEPHERD NEAME

A story that's been brewing for 300 years

THEO BARKER

Professor Emeritus of Economic History

in the University of London

Published by Granta Editions
25–27 High Street, Chesterton, Cambridge CB4 1ND,
United Kingdom.

Granta Editions is a wholly owned imprint of Book Production Consultants plc

First published in 1998.
© 1998 Shepherd Neame
17 Court Street, Faversham, Kent ME13 7AX.

A CIP catalogue record for this book is available from the British Library.

ISBN 1 85757 062 6

PICTURE ACKNOWLEDGEMENTS

The author and publishers are grateful to the following for permission to reproduce photographs and illustrations:

p.1 Public Record Office; p.5 Birmingham City Archives [Document ref.: PF46]; p.13, 19,
39 Peter Kennett; p.21, 37, 49, 59, 71, 89 Canterbury Cathedral Archives; p.60 Imperial
War Museum, London; p.66–7 Whitstable Museum & Gallery (Douglas West Collection);
p.101 *The Independent*/Peter Macdiarmid.

All other pictures were provided by Shepherd Neame Ltd.

The publishers wish to thank John Owen for kindly researching and supplying information for the maps on pages 21, 37, 49, 59, 71, 89.

Grateful thanks also to Peter Smith and Barry Duffield, who provided photography for this
book.

Every effort has been made to obtain permission for the reproduction of the illustrations
and photographs in this book; apologies are offered to anyone whom it has not been possible to contact.

Designed by Peter Dolton.
Design, editorial and production in association with
Book Production Consultants plc, 25–27 High Street, Chesterton,
Cambridge CB4 1ND, United Kingdom.
Reprographics in Great Britain by Centre Media, London, United Kingdom.
Printed in Great Britain by Jarrold Book Printers, Thetford, Norfolk, United Kingdom.

CONTENTS

FOREWORD

It is a great privilege for me to write the foreword to this book celebrating our 300th anniversary. On 28 August 1948, in one of the first celebrations after the end of the Second World War, Shepherd Neame held a 250th anniversary dinner for all the Company's employees and many of its major customers. Although still a schoolboy, I was invited to attend and I was left in no doubt that I was expected to follow in the family footsteps with a lifelong career in the Company.

In the 50 years since that dinner, vast changes have occurred which could never have been envisaged. I feel particularly honoured to have been a member of the Company for much of that time and to have been able, along with many others who have had long-term connections, to ensure its continuation as a family business.

It has taken five years to unravel the history of the Brewery, the lack of records making the early years particularly difficult to research. I would like to pay tribute to the author for his tenacity in tackling the records, and to all those who have given so much assistance to the project.

I hope you will find the history of Shepherd Neame as fascinating as I have found the challenge of work over the last 43 years.

R H B Neame

July 1998

PREFACE

A short history of Faversham Brewery was published in 1948. Modestly described as a 'souvenir brochure', it is now something of a collector's item.

Two good reasons for producing another little book on the subject, if only to make further details of the growth of this successful family business readily available to another generation of readers:

1. More sources of information have become available both among the Brewery's own records and elsewhere during the past half century. They add considerably to what was previously known about the business and to our understanding of how and why it has continued to flourish and grow when so many others have fallen victim to mergers.

2. Since 1948 mergers have been particularly pronounced in British business generally and the brewing industry in particular. Between 1954 and 1993 the number of brewing companies in Britain fell from 305 to 65 and the number of breweries they owned from 479 to 94. From these takeovers Shepherd Neame has emerged with conspicuous success, much to the advantage of those whose livelihood depended upon their employment by the company both in Faversham and elsewhere. Shepherd Neame Ltd is much more widely known at the end of the century, and its beers consumed much further afield now than was the case 50 years ago. The company has won prizes in international competitions so far away as Las Vegas.

SHEPHERD NEAME – AND MARES

It will be helpful to say something about the Shepherd and Neame relationship at the outset. Despite the present company name, the Shepherd and Neame families were engaged together in its management for only 13 years in its long history stretching back more than three centuries. The last member of the Shepherd family ceased to be involved over a century ago, in 1877. The first certain evidence of the Neame family's involvement is to be found in the acceptance of a bill by Percy Beale Neame on 11 October 1864. He had become a partner at the beginning of that month and the firm was for a time known as Shepherd, Mares & Neame.

Few people will ever have heard of John Henry Mares. The souvenir brochure of 1948 gives him only a passing mention. Yet he played a most important part in the creation of the present business and was responsible for the introduction to it of the Neame family, for he had married Percy Neame's sister. The Neames were already substantial property owners in the district. Charles Neame of Harefield Court, for instance, and John Neame of Selling Court were considered the most extensive hop growers in East Kent. Frederick Neame farmed at Macknade. Successive members of another branch of the family acted as agents to Lord Sondes's Lees Court Estate. They also managed Otterden for Sir Granville Wheler as well as Nash Court which was owned by H.A. Milles Lade.

John Henry Mares came from Maidstone and belonged to a well-to-do family of jewellers there. His father was several times its mayor. He himself had attended the Proprietory School with James Tassell. Tassell, after leaving school served his articles with a solicitor in Hythe before becoming, in 1842, partner in the leading legal firm in Faversham, headed by a member of the Shepherd family, Julius Gaborian Shepherd, whose father, a solicitor in the town before him, had not gone into the Brewery. Julius Gaborian Shepherd served as clerk to the Pavement Commissioners, borough treasurer and coroner. James Tassell wisely consolidated his position in the firm of Shepherd & Tassell by marrying one of Julius Gaborian's daughters, Charlotte Ann.

It was James Tassell who came to the rescue of the Shepherd family's brewing interests at a time of national financial crisis at the end of the 1840s when, as we shall see, a non-Shepherd partner in the business had decided to withdraw from it. At this juncture Tassell persuaded his former school friend to leave Maidstone and to put about £5,000 (about a quarter of a million pounds in modern money) into Faversham Brewery which then became known as Shepherd & Mares.

CHAPTER ONE

Founding Fathers

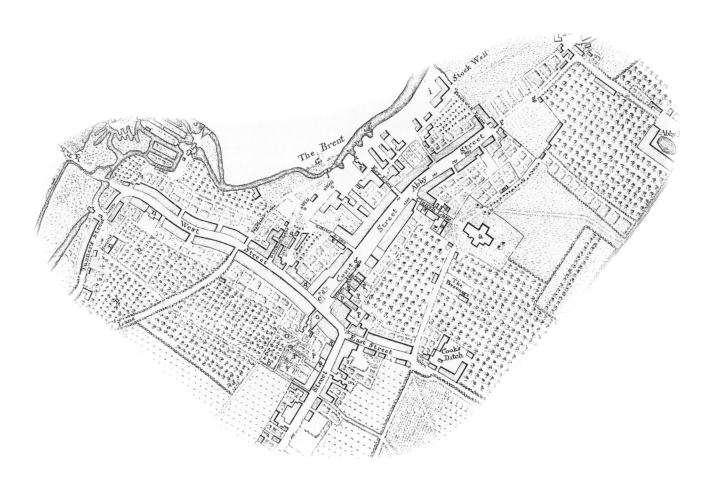

A plan of the town of Faversham, 1774

TRADITION has it that Faversham Brewery dates back to 1698. It was founded neither by a Shepherd, nor by a Neame, but by Richard Marsh who, like the Neames and the Shepherds, came from a well-established East Kent family. One of his forebears was Anne, sister of Sir Francis Nethersole of Nethersole House, who married into the Marsh family of Brandred in Acrise. A contemporary, Thomas Marsh (1666–1739), was a lieutenant colonel in the Cinque Ports militia, Captain of Sandown Castle and Deputy Lieutenant of the county.

Richard Marsh was also in the militia and came to be known in Faversham as Captain Richard Marsh. He wrote an eye-witness account of James II's arrival in Faversham in December 1688, subsequently printed as an appendix to Jacob's *History of Faversham*. This strongly suggests that his connection with Faversham Brewery may have occurred before 1698. Certainly the Faversham Wardmote Books show that Marsh was already paying the largest brewer's fine in Faversham by 25 March 1678. He paid 33s 4d, whereas the other 23 men and 3 women named were all paying a mere 4s 6d and could have been little more than licensed victuallers, paying for brewing rights on their own premises.

Richard Marsh and the beginnings of Faversham Brewery

A large common brewery in Faversham was, therefore, in being at least 20 years before 1698. In the absence of any extant deeds or even a relevant abstract of title, we cannot be sure of how the date 1698 originated, but it is probable that the main brewery had previously existed somewhere else in Faversham and moved to its present site in 1698. We do know, however, that 'established 1698' appeared in an advertisement for Faversham Brewery in the *Kentish Gazette* of 11 April 1865, the first time it appeared under the name of Shepherd Neame & Company. This was over 160 years after 1698, by which time any oral tradition which may have survived, passed on from generation to generation of the Marsh and Shepherd families to the Neames, had probably become somewhat vague. Suffice it to say that, while it is always possible that the then ambitious and rapidly growing Shepherd Neame business may have owned deeds which we no longer possess, the Wardmote Books now make it quite clear that they could quite legitimately have taken their claim back at least 20 years further. This would give Shepherd Neame a greater claim to distinction on grounds of age for, according to the excise returns, there were already 746 common brewers in the kingdom.

Silvester Marsh sells to Samuel Shepherd

Captain Richard Marsh died in or before 1727. A court case on 4 October of that year showed that Faversham Brewery, which then included a malting and a dwelling house attached in Court Street West, was settled upon his widow. His daughter, Silvester Marsh, 'daughter and heir at law of her late father Richard Marsh', sold the property, similarly described, to Samuel Shepherd who, another deed tells us, was in possession by 12 October 1741. She herself was buried at Faversham Parish Church in 1742.

Captain Richard Marsh, founder of the Faversham Brewery.

The Shepherds were a family of substance, owning land at Great Mongeham near Deal. Samuel Shepherd had come to Faversham in the early 1730s, if not before, and was already involved in malting. According to an advertisement in the *Kentish Post* of 13 January 1732/3, he 'makes and sells superfine Pale Malt and also Brown Malt, Wholesale or Retail at reasonable prices'. He could even go so far as to describe himself then as 'Brewer at Faversham'. The borough records reveal him paying £20 rackrent on a brewhouse in the following year, 1734. By then he had already established himself in the town. He served as mayor in 1733 and became mayor again on two subsequent occasions in later years.

Faversham, with its good underground sources of water, containing the appropriate quantities of calcium needed for making good beer, had probably been a source of ale for centuries. In the late seventeenth century it became an increasingly important source of beer, supplying not only the growing little town but also its hinterland to the south where the population was also increasing.

The road southward had an easy gradient, readily negotiated by horse-drawn vehicles. Faversham was also the harbour through which goods from London were forwarded to Ashford.

Faversham beer formed part of this growing traffic; while London and its huge metropolitan market remained the country's main brewing centre, Faversham was far enough away to develop a niche market for beer in parts of Kent. These included some London beers for which Faversham Brewery acted as agent.

Edward Rigden also started to brew in the town at this time, possibly at first in Preston Street before moving to the east of Court Street, opposite Faversham Brewery with which his own brewery shared the plentiful under-ground water supply. The Rigdens were already major brewers in Canterbury, but just how large their operation in Faversham was, or how closely connected to Canterbury, is not clear, though there can be no doubt of Edward Rigden's prominence in Faversham, for he served as mayor in 1744, 1751 and 1757. Rigdens were to expand their Faversham brewery very considerably, and concentrate there, after 1870.

Samuel Shepherd brought new drive to the business. He acquired his own pubs in Faversham as well as supplying customers and various public houses owned by others direct from the Brewery. When Julius Shepherd, who had joined his father in the management in 1755, inherited the business in 1770, it included the Castle in West Street, the Three Tuns in Tanner Street, the Ship in the market place (acquired from the Ruck family) and the Red Lion, adjoining the Brewery. To these Julius added the Royal Oak in South Street, the Queen's Head, next to the Ship, and the Mermaid and the Anchor in Abbey Street. So was started the process of acquiring tied outlets to make the Brewery's output more readily available.

Julius Shepherd – and the steam engine

Julius Shepherd had other interests outside the Brewery. In 1763 he was co-founder and first Worshipful Master of the Lodge of Harmony which was to become – and remains to this day – a significant institution in Faversham. In 1787 he bought land in Herne Hill which he farmed. He fathered a large family, part of which established a legal practice in Faversham which passed into the possession of the Tassell family.

Two of Julius Shepherd's sons in due course joined him at the Brewery. Charles (born 1773) unfortunately died at the age of 29. Henry (1781–1862) succeeded when Julius died in 1819. Henry Shepherd was long remembered in Faversham for continuing to wear knee breeches long after they had passed out of fashion. His son, also called Henry (1816–77), was the last of the Shepherds to be actively involved in management.

Julius Shepherd, a key figure in the history of the Brewery, purchased a 'sun and planet' steam engine from Boulton & Watt in 1789. According to their Soho engine book, it was the first Boulton & Watt machine to be installed in any brewery outside London and was used to do the work of malt

The 'sun and planet' steam engine, bought by Julius Shepherd in 1789, helped to modernise the Brewery. It was the first Boulton & Watt machine to be fitted in any brewery outside London.

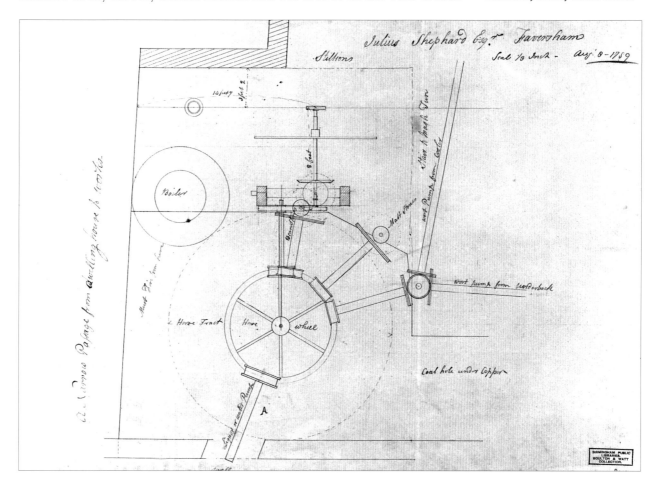

grinding and pumping previously undertaken by horses. The Brewery thereafter made much of this symbol of modernisation and progress, proudly describing itself as the Faversham Steam Brewery.

High taxation and hard times

During the first 25 years of the nineteenth century, however, as the national barrelage totals for both strong and table beer tell us, the country's brewers were failing to develop their businesses in spite of general economic growth and rising population. As Kent witnessed much rural unrest arising from low earnings as well as the threat of labour-saving threshing machines, there is every reason to believe that, despite Julius Shepherd's resourcefulness, Faversham Brewery suffered as much as any other. At the heart of the trouble was the higher rates of taxation needed to finance the Napoleonic wars and, after 1815, to service the wartime loans.

The two most important items of daily diet in these days were bread and beer. Bread baking was a relatively simple process carried out in numerous bakeries throughout the kingdom as well as at home; so it was impractical for the excise authorities to raise duty on all this widely scattered output. Beer brewing, on the other hand, was a much more attractive tax collecting proposition: it was more sophisticated, carried out in fewer places and very rarely at home.

Excise duties on beer and its ingredients, malt and hops, made a significant contribution to the total British tax yield. In 1805, for instance, excise duties of all sorts brought in £22.5m, which was then getting on for half of national taxation *from all sources*. Of the £22.5m, beer, malt and hops contributed just under £10m. Spirit duties added a further £5m. Most of the malt liquor duties were borne by the common brewers and brewing victuallers. The large mansions of the well-to-do, which often included their own brewhouses, avoided almost all of these duties on payment of a minimum fee; but very few of their owners made their own malt and could not escape paying duty on that. They and their servants and harvesters did well; but most people who drank at, or bought from, the local pub, had to pay very high, excise-induced prices. The high prices inevitably restricted sales.

These prices were soon starting to cause national concern and to be discussed in parliament. Beer was seen as a patriotic drink. At that time it depended on home-grown ingredients. Its consumption was of importance to farmers and landowners alike. In many rural areas a popular toast was: 'Here's health to the brewer and God speed the plough.'

Beer encouraged as a temperance drink The most immediate way to reduce prices and stimulate consumption was, obviously, to reduce taxation. The Country Brewers' Society was formed in 1822 and an Act of the following year halved the duty on an intermediate beer, less alcoholic than the stronger variety. Its effect was, not surprisingly, minimal; but it was a start.

Of much greater consequence, harmful to brewers, was the reduction, from 11s 9d to 7s per gallon, of the spirit duties in 1825 which resulted in a quick doubling of spirit sales and a further reduction of beer consumption. Drunkenness, however, increased and this led to greater support for beer as, relatively, a temperance drink.

A more effective measure was passed in 1830. This was the Beer Act – which removed all duties on beer and allowed any ratepayer to open a beerhouse to sell beer on or off the premises on payment of a licence fee of two guineas direct to the excise authorities, opening hours being set between 5 a.m. and 10 p.m. The duties were, however, retained on malt, thus catching all brewers, including the well-to-do in their large mansions. Over 24,000 beerhouses were opened within six months and 46,000 within eight years. Greater competition within the trade resulted in much rejoicing in pubs throughout the land and the Rev Sydney Smith's well-remembered comment: 'Everyone is drunk. Those who are not singing are sprawling. The sovereign people are in a beastly state.' But control of beerhouses was tightened in subsequent legislation and drunkenness was considerably reduced by the end of the decade.

While the new beerhouses competed with the older pubs, in some of which Faversham Brewery had a financial interest, the beerhouses nevertheless increased the number of outlets for the Brewery's products. The greater demand for beer encouraged agricultural production and earnings in its rural market area. Economic circumstances for brewers improved, though what was true for Faversham Brewery was also true for its more recent Rigden rival over the road. It was a highly competitive situation.

Shepherd & Hilton   During the more difficult earlier decades of the nineteenth century the Shepherds were no doubt encouraged by support from another prominent local family, the Hiltons, though this alliance was to give rise to subsequent difficulty.

In 1802 Giles Hilton (1779–1867) married Julius Shepherd's niece, Mary. Giles's father had been a founding partner in the Commercial Bank of Faversham in 1796 and Giles had succeeded him there. Now Giles became a partner in the Brewery also, and the brewing business of Shepherd & Hilton weathered the difficult years well enough.

The Brewery's first letter books, 1844–53, enable us to get a clearer idea of Shepherd & Hilton's day-to-day business in the years before the railway reached Faversham. Horse-drawn drays carried the firm's beer over good, solid roads along the coast to the east and west, as well as to Canterbury, to Ashford and beyond. They even went so far as Sandwich. 'The distance is great,' wrote one of the partners, thereby reflecting ideas of distance in those days. 'But,' he added, emphasising the firm's wish to continue growing, 'we are anxious to keep up as extended a connexion as we can.' The firm had an interest, with others, in several pubs in Dover. Although the partners claimed that 'it hardly answers our purpose' to send beer as far as Woodchurch, they nevertheless sent some there and a house was acquired at Ruckinge. The Brewery was becoming an increasingly important property owner.

To find tenants for this increasing number of houses was a major concern. Sometimes good men – and women – came with the houses acquired; but the partners often found the existing tenants unsatisfactory. They sometimes dismissed them, summarily: in the case of the Shakespeare, Canterbury, they told the existing tenant that they 'felt obliged by your leaving tomorrow morning as early as you conveniently can' so that they could immediately install their own people. Sometimes would-be tenants wrote in offering their services, which called for their backgrounds to be investigated. On one occasion when a young man sought a tenancy, the partners, in writing to a relative for a character reference, indicated, in the most general terms, the qualities they sought. 'Is he a person you can recommend as steady, sober and who will make a good tenant?'

The partners bargained hard when they were buying premises. Surveyors acting for them quoted a low price and the partners offered a little more so as to seem generous, while at the same time stressing that the property concerned was 'dilapidated' (an adjective much favoured by them) and required considerable expenditure to bring it up to standard.

When the price was agreed, there was always scope to haggle over the expenses incurred, as one of the partners explained to the intermediary who had put Faversham Brewery in touch with the vendors:

> We are much obliged to you for the offer of the House at King's Down. If we can become purchasers upon the usual terms of the vendors making a good title and the purchasers recalling the expenses attending the conveyance, we should be happy to treat; but we should not like to undertake to pay all expenses attending the sale and transfer which…are, of course, very considerable.

Once bought, the houses required careful maintenance. Towards the end of September 1847, for instance, with winter approaching, the firm became concerned about the leads in the windows of the King's Arms, Canterbury, and the lack of shutters. The work was doubly urgent for, it was also noted, 'long days for tradesmen's work are decreasing'. Other matters – such as water pouring from a nearby property on to a yard behind one of their public houses, requiring the offending party to put up guttering – frequently took up much of the partners' time.

They, not the tenants, were responsible at law for seeing that their houses were kept in an orderly manner. 'We have complaints from the clergyman of your parish,' they wrote to one of their tenants in Borden, on the southwestern fringes of Sittingbourne, 'that the Tanners Arms is not a well conducted house and he attributes this to you having some persons living with you who encourage irregularity. As we do not wish to lose the licence of your house, we must request that you will immediately get rid of those persons or we shall be under the necessity of giving you notice.' When the vicar wrote again, however, a little later, in terms which were far from polite, a partner took a sterner line with him!

> We are at all times obliged for information respecting the misconduct of our Publicans, as it is our determination as is in our power to prevent their allowing their houses to be an annoyance to the neighbourhood in which they are situated; and the good feeling which (with the exception of the parish of Borden) exists between our Publicans and the inhabitants generally of those parishes in which we have property is, I think, fair proof that our influence is successfully exerted.
>
> But, while thanking you for the inference of improper hours that are kept at The British Queen, we can but express our regret that you should think it necessary to write in terms which, to say the least of them, are extremely uncourteous.

Constant vigilance as property owners

By the middle of the nineteenth century the firm had reached a powerful position. The partners had no hesitation in speaking their mind. Very low in the pecking order came builders invited to repair or maintain their houses. The words 'surprised' or even 'astonished' were frequently used when the first bids came in. The real gem, however, added: 'We trust that, should you find when it is done, your calculations were wrong, you will send us your bill accordingly.'

The partners spent much time keeping outgoings to a minimum. When a bakehouse – 'dilapidated' – behind one of their premises was removed, it was taken apart carefully so that the building materials could be reused elsewhere. On another occasion they agreed to a small fence just over 3 ft high to be newly built in front of a pub, provided the artisan involved agreed to 'repair the other with the old stuff'. He was told to 'proceed with the same at your convenience and not do more than you think necessary'. 'The price we pay for hanging paper of that description is 9d a piece,' a decorator was told in 1847. 'We presume this will be your price.'

The partners lent money to new tenants – at interest – to enable them to purchase fixtures and fittings. They also lent to customers on occasion. To this extent the Brewery performed the function of a bank as well as a supplier of beer. Many people were reluctant payers and much of the partners' time was taken up with chasing debts as well as payment for beer received. In the mid-1840s some of these debts had been owed for two or three years and the loans dated back to the early years of the decade which, we now know, saw the worst depression of the whole of the nineteenth century.

The firm grew impatient with backsliders. 'Have you not broken your promise?' a tenant was asked. 'Unless you remit to us one half of the sum you owe us a fortnight from this day, we shall leave the matter entirely in our lawyer's hands.' To Mrs Norman of Greenstreet, Teynham, however, a much more conciliatory approach was adopted. The partners were 'sorry to be obliged again to apply to Mrs Norman for the payment of her account and now beg to inform her that if the account is not paid in the course of a few days they should be under the necessity of placing it in the lawyer's hands'. A particularly recalcitrant payer happened to be none other than the vicar of Borden who had complained about the houses in his parish. He was dealt with much more tersely. 'We think it strange you should compel us to write so often for your account due for beer. If the sum is not paid by the end of next week, we must decline supplying more beer and resort to other means to get the account settled.'

The worst position, however, occurred when a tenant fell behind in payment, managed his pub badly and was, therefore, unlikely ever to pay his debts to the Brewery. The Castle Inn, Ashford, provided an example of this. On 19 May 1853 the firm wrote to Philip Mein, the tenant:

We are sorry to be under the necessity of giving you notice to leave our house, as we feel satisfied you are not getting a living at it and only spending your own money, and ours too, besides which we find the House is not conducted to the satisfaction of the inhabitants generally. Therefore on consideration we feel assured you will think, as we do, that it is policy on your part to leave and get into something smaller, which Mrs Mein is more competent to manage, before your property is entirely wasted, and we have no doubt we shall meet with a House of that kind to offer you before a great while when you would be less annoyed by business matters than at your present House…You will see by the enclosed notice we have given you till 11 October next that you, as well as we ourselves, will have longer time to look for something suitable for you.

Hoping this arrangement will meet your views.

The exact wording of the notice read:

To Philip Mein of the Castle Inn, Ashford
We hereby give you notice to quit and deliver on 11th of October next the peaceable and quiet possession of all the Messuage and Tenement with appurtenances thereto known by the sign of the Castle Inn in the Town of Ashford which you rent and hold of us.

Sale of London porter and return of casks

This correspondence also shows that Faversham Brewery had been marketing for some time, through its sales outlets, not only its own products but also London-brewed porter. It complained to Trumans early in 1845 of a Mr Sharpe who had been selling Truman porter in Faversham and Whitstable. Having thanked Trumans for their 'early attention to our wishes', the partners went on to explain:

The complaint against Mr Sharpe was not so much that he undersold us but that he was sending porter into part of our district which, of course, must be injurious to our Agency. Both Faversham and Whitstable are places covered in your original agreement with Mr Shepherd and consequently Mr Sharpe cannot complain at our wishing you to stop his sending porter to those places.

A letter to a customer a few months later explained the terms on which London porter, sent to Faversham from London by water, was ordered weekly:

We should be happy to supply you with porter on the London Terms. Shipped at the wharf you may have it at 33s. p.barrel and allow 5 per cent for cash as you now pay. We hope you will have at least two Barrels at a time as it will put them to great inconvenience to take one Barrel. The risks of the casks being returned will rest with yourself.

We write for our porter every Thursday and should wish you to let us know the day before if you can.

Responsibility for the return of casks and barrels frequently cropped up in correspondence. On one occasion a customer – at Appledore – gave particular cause for annoyance. He failed to sign his remittance, returned unsold beer produced at another brewery and sent back damaged casks. From the mild tone of the partner's reply, he must have been in a particularly good mood that day:

The waste you sent back is not of our brewery and perfectly valueless to us. Therefore if you think it worth the expense of carriage back, we will send it. If not, we must send it down the gutter. We have also to complain of the manner in which our last casks came home – hoops off and musty – and if the next parcel should come home in the same way, we must charge you the expense of cooperage etc.

Faversham Creek, pictured here at the turn of the century, was used to transport goods from London to Ashford via Faversham. The Brewery once received deliveries of malt by barge at its own wharf. By the end of the 1850s, however, even with steamboats providing quicker transport, water communication was replaced by a much faster rail service.

High prices claimed for quality beer

Writing to a customer in January 1848 in order to explain why Faversham Brewery charged 62s per cask, one of the partners justified this on grounds of quality: 'We buy the best of barley and manufacture in the best way possible.' Good quality barley, however, varied considerably in price from harvest to harvest and was often cheaper to bring to Kent from elsewhere. In 1847, for instance, the Brewery bought from a merchant in Great Yarmouth – 350 quarters at 50s 6d free on board – 'and hope that it will be quite equal to sample'. It may have been the first order, for the merchant had to be told that river dues amounted to 5d a ton on the registered tonnage and the steam tug, needed for towing up the creek, added a further 2d per ton. The year before, however, an offer from Garrards of Colchester at 34s 6d a ton was said to be 'too high'. 'The best barley in this neighbourhood is fetching 33s; and if extraordinarily good 34s is given.' In subsequent years, however, Garrards were frequent suppliers.

Within its sales area the Brewery had 'understandings' with competitors which, presumably, were reciprocated. In 1852, for instance, it was interested in acquiring an outlet at Shadoxhurst which, it told the owner, rather disparagingly, hoping to strike an advantageous price, 'with some few alterations and improvements…might be made a tolerable good house'. 'But,' the partner added, 'before going into the matter with you, I think it right to say there exists at present a very good understanding between Mr Elliott of Ashford and ourselves and we are unwilling to interfere with his trade unnecessarily. I therefore told him the offer you had made us and said we were willing to give it up to him if he could make a satisfactory arrangement with you for it. If not, we shall be willing at once to treat for it.'

John Mares to the rescue

The later 1840s saw a period when various businesses throughout the kingdom got into financial difficulties and a number of them went bankrupt. Faversham Brewery did not escape unscathed. It ran short of cash and on 24 November 1847 had to raise £3,000 by mortgaging a large part of its extensive property to James Blaxland of Tonge. (It was not repaid until December 1863.) Matters were not helped when Charles J. Hilton decided to withdraw from the business, taking his partnership capital with him. The firm's customers were begged to settle their accounts promptly. 'Owing to Mr Hilton going out of the concern,' Henry Shepherd wrote to one of them on 1 February 1848, 'I am now much pressed and must beg your earliest attention to the account.'

Just why Hilton chose this particularly awkward time to embarrass his partners is not at all clear. We know that he had interests in cement works in the locality as well as in one of the Faversham banks. He may have needed the cash to support any of these – or other interests such as further calls on railway shares.

The significance of John Henry Mares's arrival at this critical juncture with his £5,000 can now be more readily appreciated. There is no reason to believe that he had any particular knowledge of brewing before his arrival in Faversham, and his marriage to Percy Beale Neame's sister was a stroke of good fortune so far as the Brewery was concerned and, in the longer run, for the Neame family. Even more important at the time was Mares's sound business sense. He foresaw the significance of the railway's belated arrival in Faversham and pressed upon his Shepherd partners the need to expand the Brewery and its malting capacity to prepare for the growth of the market along the railway in the direction of London. It is in this sense Mares can be said to have played a major part in transforming the business from a Kent niche operation into a more widely ranging modern concern.

In 1853 the Brewery was still owned mainly by the Shepherd family. Henry Shepherd senior ('knee breeches') held a 50 per cent share and his son, Henry junior, the last of the Shepherd partners (died 1877) 25 per cent. This left Mares with the remaining 25 per cent. They were ably assisted by their salaried general manager, William Maile. When he joined the business is not known; but he was certainly signing letters on its behalf in 1857 and worked there until the time of his death in 1885. He played an active

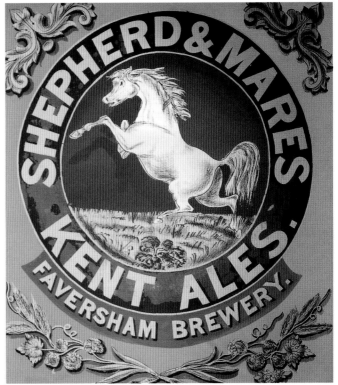

An early advertisement for Shepherd & Mares, the name the Brewery adopted in about 1848 with the arrival of John Henry Mares.

A story that's been brewing for 300 years

part in the town as a committee member of Faversham Library and Scientific Institution and as clerk to the Poor Law Guardians. We get a glimpse of him in advancing years. A partner, writing in 1881 to a customer whom he was to meet in London described him as 'Our Mr Maile, who has the running of this business…is stout, with a long grey beard and moustache' – in fact the epitome of a Victorian worthy.

The trains arrive late at Faversham

An early photograph of Court Street, Faversham, dating from 1852. The figure on the far right is thought to be Henry Shepherd senior wearing his trade-mark knee breeches.

The reason why Faversham had no railway connection until 1858, much more than a decade after Ashford, Canterbury and the coastal towns of Margate, Ramsgate and Deal to the east of it, was partly due to the policies of the South Eastern Railway and partly due to opposition from the propertied

men of Kent who lived near the route of the proposed line as it ran east from Strood. Not least there was the cost of building a railway bridge alongside the road bridge over the Medway.

When the South Eastern first connected London to Dover, it ran down the London & Brighton Railway, opened in 1841, as far as Redstone Hill (now Redhill) before striking off due east in a dead straight line across the Weald to Ashford (1842), Folkestone (1843) and Dover (1844). From Ashford a line branched out in a northeasterly direction to serve Canterbury and Ramsgate from where it ran north to Margate and, in the following year, south to Sandwich and Deal.

Having reached Canterbury and the East Kent coast by the branch from Ashford, the South Eastern considered that it had spent enough. Traffic from Rochester, Chatham and Gillingham could reach the railway easily over the Medway road bridge. Places to the east like Sittingbourne and Faversham could make do with water communication which had already been speeded up by steamboats. By the later 1850s, however, even the previously hostile propertied men of Kent were having second thoughts as they saw rival fruit growers south of the Downs getting their produce more quickly to market in London by railway. They wished to see North Kent's railway gap filled. Parliamentary sanction for a railway between Strood and Canterbury, to be built by the East Kent Railway Company, was granted in 1853, but building proceeded slowly. Faversham was not connected with Chatham until January 1858, nor with Strood and the South Eastern's North Kent line until the following March.

Shepherd & Mares had its sights on the London market even before the railway had crossed the Medway, though whether its beer reached Strood by road or whether it was sent to London by water, is not known. There is no doubt at all, however, that an advertisement in the *Faversham Gazette* on 11 April 1857 announced that 'from the frequent application for their Ales in London' Shepherd & Mares had opened 'commodious stores at Red Lion Street, Borough, which are superintended by Mr Shepherd [almost certainly Henry Shepherd junior] and any orders addressed to him will receive prompt attention'. The subsequent opening of the railway from Faversham made it easier to send Faversham beer to London, though nothing further is heard of the stores in Red Lion Street, Borough.

A story that's been brewing for 300 years

Faversham became an important railway junction as the railway to Dover, via Canterbury, was opened between 1860 and 1861, and along the coast to Whitstable, Herne Bay and Margate between 1860 and 1863. Much more important, however, was the successful escape from the haughty South Eastern's stranglehold between Strood and London when, after a complex concatenation of independent ventures, the pitiful and powerless East Kent Railway, having rechristened itself the London, Chatham & Dover, gained access to London in 1860 via a line which took a more southerly route via Swanley, St Mary Cray and Bromley.

The Brewery takes advantage of the new transport

Shepherd & Mares's list of bills payable show that it was spending considerable sums on extending its operations in Faversham at the end of the 1850s when the railway was providing new outlets in the London direction. Nearly £6,300 (some £315,000 in modern money) was paid to two Canterbury building firms in 1859 and 1860 and this rose by £4,000 in

Faversham's first railway station, seen here in 1880. The opening of the railway to Faversham in 1858 allowed Shepherd & Mares to transport goods more easily to its London outlets.

Horse-drawn drays carried the Brewery's beer along the coast, and even as far as Canterbury and Ashford, before the railway finally crossed the Medway in 1858. They were still used for shorter journeys until the 1960s! Left, a Shepherd Neame dray outside the Dover Castle Inn, Teynham, in 1903.

1861. In that year, ten monthly payments – totalling £2,180 – were paid to a firm up in Leith, David McLaren & Co.

In 1861 Shepherd & Mares's bitter sold at 1s per gallon for cash, but in the following year the Brewery was still stressing the importance of its Kent niche market. It advertised that its stock pale and other ales 'obtained great celebrity and are so extensively patronised in Canterbury, Maidstone, Dover, Hythe, Ashford, Faversham, Sittingbourne, Ramsgate and other towns in Kent'. Because of the increased sales in this area from the beginning of September 1861 regular deliveries to Canterbury were to be made every Monday and Thursday, to Whitstable on Tuesday and Friday, to Herne Bay on Wednesday and to Sittingbourne and Milton every day of the week. Shepherd & Mares's agents existed not only in Maidstone and Ashford but also in Hythe, Lenham, Sheerness and Smeeth.

These deliveries were still made by horse-drawn drays; but soon after that the Brewery was taking advantage of the newly arrived railway. In April 1865 Faversham Brewery, described as 'East India Pale Ale Brewers', begged to call special attention to 'their FAMILY BITTER BEER which from the delicacy of its flavour and pureness of its tonic qualities has gained so great a reputation in the estimation of the public; and also their STOCK AND MILD ALES which they are now sending out in high perfection'. All these inviting brews were now being sold from stores at Bromley as well as at Canterbury, Ramsgate and Sheerness. The Bromley stores were located at the Town Hall, and the agent, R. Cooper, had his office in the market place. Customers were reminded that the Brewers were agents for Meux & Co.'s celebrated London stout and porter which could be obtained from Faversham or from any of the stores.

The death in 1862 of the elder ('knee breeches') Henry Shepherd, the major shareholder, was not unexpected, for he was 82 years old. Faversham was his native town. He had lived there all his life and was buried in the graveyard of the parish church, a plaque in the choir of the church itself providing information about him. Although his son, Henry, was not a businessman of the same calibre, the firm's expansion continued satisfactorily with Mares as the real driving force. Percy Beale Neame joined them in October 1864.

Mares's death on 28 December 1864 at the early age of 45 was a damaging and quite unexpected blow even though he did not leave the firm in the same financial plight as Hilton had done. By a codicil to his will dated two days before his death, Mares instructed his trustees to allow his share to remain in the business for such time as the trustees thought fit. The freehold value of the firm, now at last Shepherd Neame, was put at £52,225 and the leasehold value at £3,974. Goodwill was a mere £2,500. The value of the whole business – brewery, public houses and stock – was after all debts had been taken into account calculated, with unbelievable accuracy, at £102,446 1s 10d (over £5m in present-day money). Henry Shepherd's share was £17,810, the Mares trustees' £18,378 and Neame's £10,034.

Percy Neame, now left unexpectedly alone with the weaker Shepherd partner, found himself suddenly confronted, at the age of 28, with the great challenge of matching the Brewery's greater capacity to the possibilities of the wider market. But he was a worthy successor to his brother-in-law who had brought him into management in the first place. During his long life Faversham Brewery came very definitely into Neame family ownership.

Henry Shepherd junior, the last of the Shepherd partners.

CHAPTER TWO

The Neames Succeed

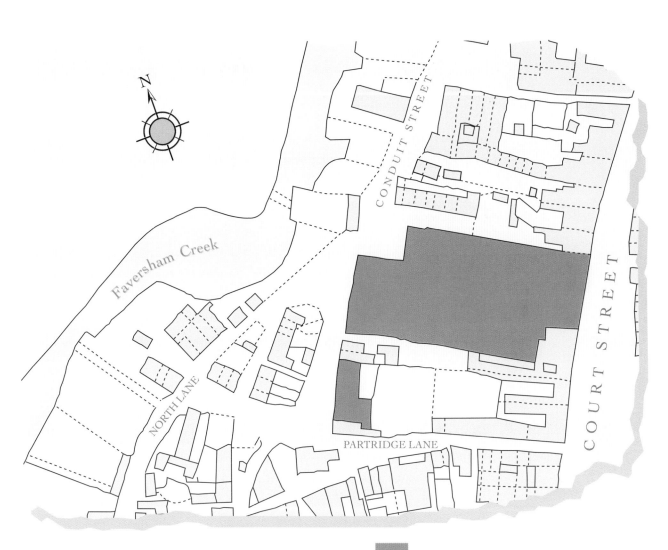

BREWERY BUILDINGS TO 1815

FROM the 1860s the changing trends in the barrelage totals enable us to take a longer view of the Brewery's different stages of growth until 1900. Barrelage grew at a very rapid rate from the low base of 13,100 in the year from October 1859 to September 1860 to 21,321 in 1863/4 as a result of investment in productive capacity before Mares's untimely death. A new mash tun was installed in September 1864, together with a new liquor tank, hop back and a 35-barrel-per-hour refrigerator to cool the hot wort before its fermentation. Fermentation capacity was also increased. This investment made greater output possible: 27,194 barrels in the following year. As returns were negligible, barrelage can be said to represent actual sales. Of the 27,194 barrels, 12,436 were described as beer, 6,081 as best beer, 2,842 as porter, some of which was brewed at Faversham and some forwarded, on behalf of London brewers. The remainder, close on 6,000 barrels, was made up of small quantities of other varieties of drink.

Greater beer output called for greater raw material input which often had to be brought from farther afield. Some barley came from Essex and even from Narborough in Norfolk. The Brewery also placed regular orders for hops so far away as Bamberg in northern Bavaria, though most of its hops came, of course, from Kent.

Barrelage was further increased to 38,251 in 1867/8 but was then held at that level for four years, as can be seen in the table on page 26. Output still totalled only 38,419 barrels in 1871/2. These were not, however, years without further investment, though, as if to bring the previous bout of productive investment to a logical conclusion, the new money was put into the building of a new office. The *Faversham Directory* of 1870 reported that in the previous year there had been built 'a handsome building on the site of the premises in Court Street, formerly in the occupation of Messrs Dan and Sons'. This formed part of what was to become the present head office.

17 Court Street, the Brewery's new office, built in 1869. Today the frontage is extended but still retains the original nineteenth century features.

By this time the Brewery had also greatly increased the number of its tied outlets. Julius Shepherd had given some impetus to this process after 1770. By the time that Percy Neame became the dominant partner, nearly a century later, the number of outlets had grown considerably and so had the geographical area in which they were located. A volume which happens to have survived at the Brewery details all repairs and redecoration undertaken at each pub, inn or store between 1871 and 1896. It shows that during the 1870s alone, no fewer than 115 different licensed premises were concerned, sometimes with cottages or other buildings attached. Faversham itself, of course, continued to be well represented and places not far away, such as the Carpenter's Arms, Eastling; the Queen's Head, Fox Inn and Dolphin (with cottages), Boughton; and the Jolly Sailors, Milton.

Shepherd Neame was also represented along the well-established route to the south, not only at the Castle at Ashford but also at the Rose & Crown and at its stores there. There were also the Bonnie Cravat at Woodchurch, the Chequers at Lenham and the Crown & Anchor at Willesborough. To the east was the Falstaff at Ramsgate – and stores there. There were also stores at Margate. Gibbs's brewery in Bridge was bought in 1876 for £1,000. The brewery was discontinued and turned into a store.

In the London direction were a depot at Farningham Road, Milton, the Beacon Court Tavern and the Monarch Inn at New Brompton, and houses and stores at Penge. Every effort was made to develop this London-bound traffic. By 1874 Shepherd Neame was running ten of its own railway wagons on the London, Chatham & Dover Railway, each of them bought for £120 and fitted with Chubb locks as a safeguard against pilfering. Each wagon carried 30 barrels of beer. In 1874 Shepherd Neame rented a shop at Victoria Station for £40 a year. It served as a West End office for a short time.

The early 1870s were boom years in England as a whole. Shepherd Neame seized every advantage of this favourable market and its numerous outlets. The Brewery's output rose to a nineteenth century peak, not reached again until the eve of the First World War: 45,046 barrels in 1873/4.

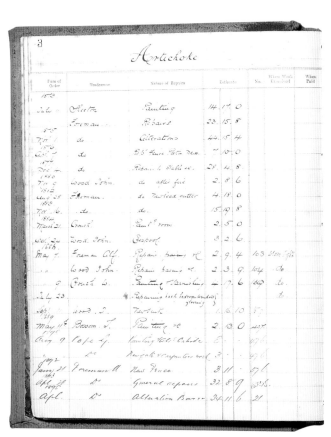

The Brewery kept detailed records of the repair and maintenance costs of each of its pubs.

Output for the next four years, to 1877/8, averaged nearly 43,000 barrels. The end of the 1870s, however, saw the slump after the boom: it witnessed, in fact, a depression the depth of which was second only to that of the early 1840s. Shepherd Neame's barrelage fell sharply, to 39,387 in 1878/9 and 36,826 in 1879/80 as production was reined back. For the rest of the century output rarely rose above 34,000 barrels, though the later 1890s at last saw the beginnings of recovery towards 40,000.

The detailed accounts do not survive from which these profit totals are derived. It is not possible, therefore, to explain the lack of correlation between

The Monarch Inn, New Brompton, Gillingham.

barrelage and net profit in certain years – from 1870/1 to 1872/3, for instance, when output grew but net profit did not; indeed it fell a little in 1872/3 when output forged ahead. It should be noted, however, that the figures are for net, not gross, profit. Although the Brewery traded as Shepherd Neame & Co., it was still an unlimited private business which could switch resources, unannounced, at will, and was not yet a registered company. The main point to be stressed, however, is that Shepherd Neame continued to make money throughout the more highly competitive last quarter of the nineteenth century by which time, because of the general fall in prices, the pound sterling was worth much more than it had been in 1870.

Hard times for brewing

The disappointing production figures of the later nineteenth century are difficult to explain. The population of England and Wales was growing at 12 per cent or more per decade and Kent's population was growing considerably faster, from 616,000 in 1851 to 1,349,000 in 1901 and 1,512,000 in 1911. (These are all totals for the ancient county of Kent, including those parts nearest London, supplied by Shepherd Neame, which became part of the new County of London at the end of the 1880s.)

Shepherd Neame output and net profit for the years ended 30 September 1867 (1866/7) to 1899/1900

	Barrelage	Net profit (£)		Barrelage	Net profit (£)
1866/7	34,450	3,030	**1883/4**	35,932	11,554
1867/8	38,251	8,529	**1884/5**	34,752	10,536
1868/9	37,933	10,344	**1885/6**	33,813	11,295
1869/70	37,330	10,315	**1886/7**	33,154	10,543
1870/1	37,328	13,951	**1887/8**	31,375	11,741
1871/2	38,419	13,911	**1888/9**	33,004	9,962
1872/3	40,377	13,413	**1889/90**	33,340	11,223
1873/4	45,046	15,542	**1890/1**	31,720	10,004
1874/5	43,454	10,809	**1891/2**	32,972	7,083
1875/6	41,933	15,498	**1892/3**	34,366	11,373
1876/7	42,295	15,842	**1893/4**	34,597	12,356
1877/8	43,502	16,648	**1894/5**	35,543	15,116
1878/9	39,387	14,519	**1895/6**	36,576	17,760
1879/80	36,826	10,577	**1896/7**	36,562	17,163
1880/1	34,353	13,230	**1897/8**	39,215	20,039
1881/2	32,451	9,652	**1898/9**	40,497	19,100
1882/3	32,258	10,104	**1899/1900**	39,612	19,132

SOURCE Shepherd Neame Company Records

In view of this increase in the number of potential beer drinkers, how are the disappointing last two decades of the nineteenth century to be explained?

The first point that needs to be made is that Shepherd Neame's experience was by no means unusual. Beer production throughout England and Wales, while increasing steadily from 16.1m barrels a year in 1855–9 to 28.2m in 1875–9, fell back to 25m in 1880–4 and 25.5m in 1885–9. It then rose slowly (27.7m 1890–4; 30.3m 1895–9). With rising real earnings, and more leisure time (shorter working days and Saturday half holidays) there were other means of spending time and money to compete with pubs: railway excursions, for instance, sports fixtures, music halls and theatres. Those who favoured less drinking (the temperance movement) or total abstinence (the teetotallers) did all they could to encourage the public to support these alternatives; and in the later nineteenth century the Liberal Party added its weight.

While all this was not encouraging to common brewers, other development in the period favoured them. Common brewers captured most of the market as private brewing in large houses was much reduced and fewer smaller individual pubs brewed their own beer, preferring to buy it in. Some of their owners, as we have seen, sold out to common brewers like Shepherd Neame. To that extent the fall in national totals reflects the departure of these smaller producers. That Faversham Brewery was producing at least 30,000 barrels a year confirms the impression already reached: that Shepherd Neame was among the larger provincial firms, the largest of all being still situated in London to cater mainly for the huge population of the metropolis and its immediate environs.

Increasing competition from W.E. and J. Rigden

The more favourable early 1870s which enabled the firm to reach its peak output of just over 45,000 barrels in 1873/4, thanks to its earlier investment in brewing capacity, also encouraged its competitor over the road, W.E. and J. Rigden, to follow suit. Faversham, not Canterbury, became the main Rigden centre. Date stones show that major extensions to the Rigden brewery building were carried out in 1874 and 1876. (A splendid building to the east, used for non-brewing purposes, and now occupied by Tesco,

Number of common brewers licensed in the United Kingdom, 1861–1914							
Barrels	**1861**	**1871**	**1881**	**1891**	**1901**	**1911**	**1914**
1,000–9,999	1,614	1,810	1,677	1,370	911	716	580
10,000–19,999	160	216	275	284	263	202	197
20,000–199,999	103	154	197	279	326	310	310
200,000–499,999	10	8	10	13	11	11	16
500,000–999,999		4	2	2	6	5	5
1,000,000–1,999,999			1	2	2	1	2
2,000,000+					1	1	1
Total	**1,887**	**2,192**	**2,162**	**1,950**	**1,520**	**1,246**	**1,111**

SOURCE Gourvish and Wilson, *British Brewing Industry (1830–1980)*, p111

A story that's been brewing
for 300 years

Percy Beale Neame joined the Brewery
in 1864 and became sole proprietor of
what was then known as Shepherd
Neame & Co. in 1877. He was the first
Neame to be a partner in what
became a family business.

followed in 1884.) This additional brewing capacity became available in the depression years at the end of the 1870s and no doubt made competition between the two Faversham firms all the fiercer in the same market area not only then but also after 1880 with the upswing of the trade cycle.

Newspaper advertisements for Rigden's Faversham beer were produced on a much more modest scale than the proud display announcements of the older Faversham Brewery. This remained true until the Rigden brewery in Faversham was enlarged in the 1870s. *Faversham News* was still carrying a very small advertisement in its issue of 11 January 1879, modestly announcing that W.E. and J. Rigden were ready to supply customers with the season's pale ale, stout and porter which could be ordered from either Faversham or Canterbury brewery. This complementary role was soon to change, however. By January 1888, as is clear from a large price list issued by W.E. and J. Rigden, the firm was then described as 'Pale Ale and Stout Brewers and Spirit Merchants, Faversham'. It also listed 11 stores and agents. They were located not only at Beer Cart Lane, Canterbury, where the earlier Rigden brewery had been situated, and in other parts of East Kent, but also at New Brompton on the London Chatham & Dover Railway into London.

William Edward Rigden (1843–1904) and John Rigden (1846–1910) were prominent figures in the area, keen hunting men who kept their horses near the brewery, behind Middle Row. As we have seen, the family also had an interest in the Faversham Commercial Bank, which also added to their local standing. Here indeed was a powerful rival to Shepherd Neame.

Years of expansion

From 1877, Percy Neame became sole proprietor of the Faversham Steam Brewery. In 1881 his eldest son, Harry Sidney Neame, after leaving Harrow and having already received some training in brewing and malting, joined the business. In 1886 his second and third sons, Arthur and Alick Percy, also joined their father. William Maile, the faithful general manager, died in 1885. His son succeeded him but left in 1893 when George Ernest Boorman, who had been working for the firm for some time, perhaps as a traveller, became general manager.

Despite increasing competition in the trade and growing influence from

Arthur Neame – Percy Beale Neame's second son – Director 1914–16.

Alick Percy Neame – Percy Beale Neame's third son – Director 1914–16.

Shepherd Neame's traction engine being driven by F. Burney. Purchased in 1874, this Aveling and Porter engine allowed the Brewery to transport heavier goods by road to its pubs and stores in towns as far as Ashford, 13 miles away.

anti-drink pressure groups, the Brewery continued to make money, with ceaseless attempts to extend its market and to increase the sale of its products over the whole range. From 1873, for instance, it sent casks of beer regularly to Colchester via London and the Great Eastern Railway. Requests came from farther afield. When one arrived from as far away as Harrogate, however, it was turned down. 'The beer could be got there,' the enquirer was told, 'but the trouble would be getting back the empty casks.' Indeed, the return of casks and the non-payment of overdue bills remained major themes of partners' correspondence in this period as they had been earlier. An item of correspondence in July 1884 indicates the complexities which sometimes arose.

> A man named Fagg from Swinfield Minnis owes us an account and Waters told me the other day he kept another Pub at Margate or Ramsgate. See if you can find him but don't see him till you hear from me as his Mother also owes an account and we want her address also.

A letter of April 1871 sent to G. Parker, the newly appointed agent at Farningham Road station, shows how far Shepherd Neame was prepared to go to find a good local representative.

We will provide a store and allow you the use of it for a nominal consider-ation, say a penny a week. We must, however, require you to keep a book containing the names of all customers for beer in order that in the event of determination of the agency by death or otherwise we may be able to trace the empty casks… The question of stores is now before the L.C. & D.R. and until we can obtain them, we must make the best arrangements we can for supplying you. We will send you a few [casks] at a time.

Yeast and spent grains

Shepherd Neame also developed a lucrative trade in yeast. We hear nothing about this before 1870, presumably because the yeast was being sold locally; but in July 1870 a yeast press was installed. In September 1872 a London yeast merchant was told that the yeast was being sent out dry at 32s 8d per cwt de-livered in boxes. It was despatched by early train from Faversham to reach London by 10 a.m. In November 1873 the following advertisement appeared in the *Bakers' Record*:

SHEPHERD NEAME & CO. BREWERS, FAVERSHAM, KENT.
(London Stores: Camberwell New Road, Nr. L.C. & D. Railway Station
and Penge Station, L.C. & D. Railway)
beg to call the attention of the Baking Trade to their celebrated
COMPRESSED YEAST
which for *colour*, *strength* and *sweetness* stands unrivalled.
It may be obtained of the principal yeast dealers in London whose
addresses will be forwarded on application.

A list of six yeast merchants in Camberwell, Peckham, Limehouse, Caledonian Road, up from King's Cross, and Cornwall Road in West London, appeared in subsequent issues of the advertisement. Yeast supplies to London were later concentrated upon one large firm, Scroggie in Caledonian Road.

In 1884 Shepherd Neame started to head its advertisements with a copy of its trade mark. The firm sent selected newspaper editors a block from which it could be reproduced. Readers were told of the 'celebrated compound yeast which, for colour, strength and sweetness stands unrivalled, being the product of

A story that's been brewing

for 300 years

Malt and Hops only (vide Trade Mark) is the secret of its superiority over yeast produced by other materials and the cause of it being so appreciated by the public'. Readers were also reminded that Shepherd Neame's 'celebrated East India Pale Ales, Stout and Porter' were also guaranteed to be brewed 'only from malt and the best East Kent hops'.

Together with yeast, the other regular by-product consisted of spent grains, the demand for which from local farmers for cattle feed always exceeded the Brewery's capacity to supply. The turnover of yeast and spent grains rose slowly, from £1,551 in 1866/7 to £1,910 in 1871/2. Then the drive to sell more yeast to London bakers had an immediate effect, turnover rising to £3,618 in 1872/3 and remaining at that higher level for the following four years for which details have survived.

Beer continued to be sent out in good condition even in the warmer summer months. Only rarely had storekeepers to be asked to switch particular consignments from family sale because they were below standard. This succinct letter sent to the storekeeper at Margate was quite unusual – poor quality was only very reluctantly admitted:

Please not to send out the following numbers (287,300,302) to a private family as they are not quite up to the mark. You can send them into the Hay or Harvest field if you have any call for beer for that purpose.

Sales up – profits down

Shepherd Neame ploughed back much profit into the business, especially in the 1890s. In 1896 and 1897 the brewing plant was further enlarged and, also in 1896, the 24-year-old Alick Neame was given responsibility for day-to-day bargaining for all wines and spirits ordered from suppliers. He had to make up his mind quickly whether to accept a discount of 1d a gallon on gin from Vauxhall Distillery and Vinegar Works (3 February 1897) or to pay £52 per pipe for 1896 vintage port free on board Oporto, being assured by the London agents that it had been many years since such a fine vintage had been produced

A Shepherd Neame price list showing its London and Penge stores.

(September 1897). A few months earlier (14 May 1897) the London agent for Charente brandy had informed him of the receipt of a telegram announcing a severe frost in the Charente which would 'seriously injure, if not destroy' that year's vintage, under which circumstances their prices of 1893, 1895 and 1896 'must be considered available from day to day'.

Alick Neame's department was located in a building which had previously been erected in Mill Place. Three years later the firm began to bottle beer for itself for the first time in a new building in Conduit Street of which Arthur Neame took charge. (Bottling had previously been undertaken by its Folkestone agent, Underwood, Penfold & Co., wine and spirit merchants.) In 1900 No. 16 Court Street was altered to match No. 17, so making a more impressive frontage to an extended head office.

In 1899 Harry Neame was paying particular attention to the purchase of malt, while his younger brothers, Alick and Arthur, were taking charge of wine and spirits and bottling. Having tested samples from Smyrna, Moravia and Spain, he placed orders for 240 quarters from Spain at 37s a ton. In the following year he ventured further afield and bought pale malt from California.

A Shepherd Neame advertisement from the late nineteenth century bearing the 'Malt and Hops only' trade mark commitment to quality.

After 1901 Harry Neame took over from his father responsibility for buying barley. He found it paid to buy this from California, too. The Rigden brewery joined him in purchasing there and the two gained a quantity advantage. Both firms were then active members of the Kent Brewers' Union, the *Brewery Guardian* of 1 March 1898 reporting that both were represented at the Union's annual meeting at 5 Victoria Street in London.

Co-operation between the two competing breweries seems to have steadied sales turnover but did not help Shepherd Neame's net profits after 1906/7. The reasons for dwindling net profit after 1906/7, and especially its collapse after 1908/9, are hard to identify. The years between 1909/10 and 1911/12 saw a cyclical upswing, reflected in the increased sales turnover. Why was this not reflected in higher, not lower, net profit – considerably lower indeed than in the years of heavy expenditure at the end of the 1890s?

It is certainly too naive to explain lower net profit in terms of Percy

Shepherd Neame's sales turnover and net profit for the years ended 30 September 1899 (1898/9) to 1912 (1911/12)

	Sales turnover (£)	Net profit (£)
1898/9	90,286	19,100
1899/1900	88,564	19,132
1900/1	93,079	18,707
1901/2	92,101	18,845
1902/3	92,871	18,021
1903/4	96,869	18,183
1904/5	97,362	18,306
1905/6	93,518	18,058
1906/7	93,833	18,401
1907/8	90,025	15,211
1908/9	88,906	15,892
1909/10	89,023	11,554
1910/11	93,535	12,426
1911/12	99,701	12,001

SOURCE Shepherd Neame Company Records

The Licensing Bill demonstration of 1908. Faversham brewers and licensees took part in a national campaign protesting against the Liberal Government's Bill to control the licensing of pubs.

Neame's growing age. He had reached 70 in 1906 and had every reason to take life easier. But this would imply that the next generation lacked ability. This was not the case. Harry Neame was to become a quite outstanding future chairman; G.E. Boorman, the general manager, and Charles Lawrence Graham, the head brewer, both experienced non-family executives, were actively supporting the business; and Arthur and Alick Neame were shaping well in developing their separate departments, as we have seen. Managerial weakness hardly seems an adequate explanation of the fall in net profit. Perhaps higher taxation was the problem. These were years when the Liberal government of 1906, even more radical after a ministerial reshuffle, was bringing in old age pension and insurance schemes and embarking on costly naval rearmament. (Insurance indeed floated in with the dreadnoughts.)

The end of an era   Percy Neame died on 5 January 1913, and was buried at Ospringe Church.

He had lived at The Mount, Ospringe. A great lover of sport, he had maintained The Mount Cricket Ground for use of the Faversham Cricket Club. Included in its fixtures was an annual match on Whit Monday, when Percy Neame's team played another eleven selected by the mayor of the borough. It was a popular event, resembling, according to the Shepherd Neame 1948 souvenir brochure, Canterbury Week in miniature. The author added:

> Percy Neame was also an ardent and generous supporter of the Tickham Hunt, and the Annual Meet of the Foxhounds at The Mount on Boxing Day was another event which attracted a large number of townspeople. The event was marked by his hospitality – ale drawn from the wood was dispensed from the paddock in front of The Mount House.

His death ended an era in which his branch of the Neame family came to dominate the business, he himself having acted as its sole proprietor since 1877.

Shepherd Neame's future was now to be dominated by the long chairmanship of Harry Neame, a worthy successor to his long dominant father.

The Mount, Ospringe, home of Percy Neame and his family, seen here in 1882.

CHAPTER THREE

Weathering the First World War

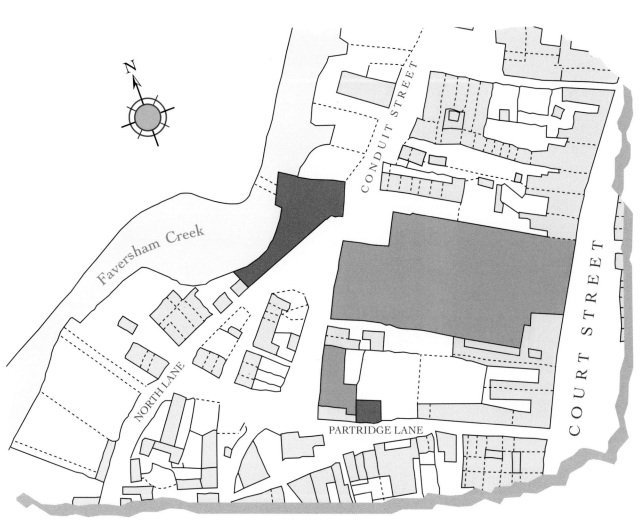

BREWERY BUILDINGS UP TO 1815   BREWERY EXPANSION 1816–1847

P ERCY Neame had fathered a large family of ten children: four sons (three of whom have been mentioned and a fourth, the youngest, Leslie Guy, born in 1892, who did not enter the firm) and six daughters. All of them, daughters as well as sons, now became shareholders in the private limited company, Shepherd Neame Ltd.

With the legal advice of George Tassell, then head of the firm of solicitors who had come to the rescue of the Brewery at the end of the 1840s, Percy Neame had devised a plan whereby all the assets of the existing business – Brewery, properties and goodwill – were transferred to the new company. Its nominal capital consisted of 100,000 £1 5 per cent cumulative preference shares (£100,000), 55,386 £1 ordinary shares (£55,386) and 166 £40 debentures (£6,640). To this, a further 10,000 £1 ordinaries were soon added. C.L. Graham, the head brewer, received 1,500 of the cumulative preference shares; Harry, Arthur and Alick Neame received 4,000 each. Leslie Guy Neame, the youngest son, who did not join the management, was allotted 2,500. The remainder were held jointly by Harry Neame, Arthur Neame and C.L. Graham. Percy Neame's six daughters each received 3,500 of the original issue of ordinaries, and Leslie Neame 5,233; but the three Neame directors did rather better (Harry 8,614, Arthur 6,371 and Alick 5,972). All ten children gained an equal (1,000) number of the subsequent issue of ordinaries.

Shepherd Neame Ltd was formed by agreement in 1914 with all ten of Percy Neame's children becoming shareholders.

The six daughters were all married. Marion, the eldest (1867–1945) had married Alaric Watts Churchward, resident in November 1914 at Mowbray, Bickley, Kent, and Florence (1870–1938) was Mrs William J. Johnston. Her husband was then a major in the army living in the staff quarters, Brompton Barracks, Chatham. Ida (1874–1951) was married to Clement Morton Loudon Cotterill of Runswick, Galton Road, Southend.

Evelyn (1877–1966) was the wife of Harold Abbott Barnes MD, whose surgery was at 19 New Road, Chatham. Madeleine (1879–1960) was married to a local farmer, Lewis Finn, whose address was given as Westwood Court, Preston next Faversham. Violet (1880–1961), the youngest daughter, was then living in Scotland, the wife of James Kerr, Rankeillor, Springfield, Cupar, Fife.

Harry Neame became chairman and managing director of the new Company, but, unlike his father, was certainly never 'sole proprietor'.

Percy Neame's outstanding debts were met by the issue of debentures to creditors; and his widow, Florence, then living at The Cottage, Weybridge, also received 40 of them. (She later married again: Major Charles Frederick Oliver Graham of Bury Grange, Alverstoke, near Gosport in Hampshire.)

G.E. Boorman was appointed company secretary from 1 July 1914 at £450 a year. The Company was formally registered on the following 11 November. The Board held its first meeting on 16 November, by which time the First World War was in its early stages.

The impact of war

Labour shortages soon became evident as some employees were offered higher wages elsewhere, or volunteered for, or were called up into, the army or navy. When, in June 1915, several boys had left the bottling store, it was decided to employ women in their place with, it was later reported, 'satisfactory results'. A month before, Douglas

Harry Sidney Neame – Percy Neame's eldest son – Brewer 1888, Managing Director 1914–40, Chairman 1913–41.

Court Street, 4 April 1915. The National Guard are seen here passing Shepherd Neame's offices. Many of Shepherd Neame's employees volunteered for, or were conscripted into, the army or navy.

Cornfoot had been appointed traveller at £98 a year, to which an extra £10 donation was soon added for his services in securing sales to the troops in the neighbourhood. His journeys had still to be made by train, for which the Company provided second-class tickets to be used only between Canterbury, Chatham and Sheerness and between Canterbury and Ashford. A year later, however, he was called up for military service whereupon the Company awarded him a gratuity of £50 a year.

In grappling with rising costs, Shepherd Neame came to depend greatly upon its auditors, the London accountants, Mason & Son, one of whose principals, Reginald Mason, advised on the allocation of annual surpluses. Earnings were good but he invariably counselled caution. When, at the first annual general meeting in August 1915, a profit of over £32,000, twice that forecast, was declared, the directors were prudently advised to treat this as a wartime windfall. The opportunity was taken to plough back some of the profit. A new mash tun and iron cold liquor back replaced the existing wooden one, which was

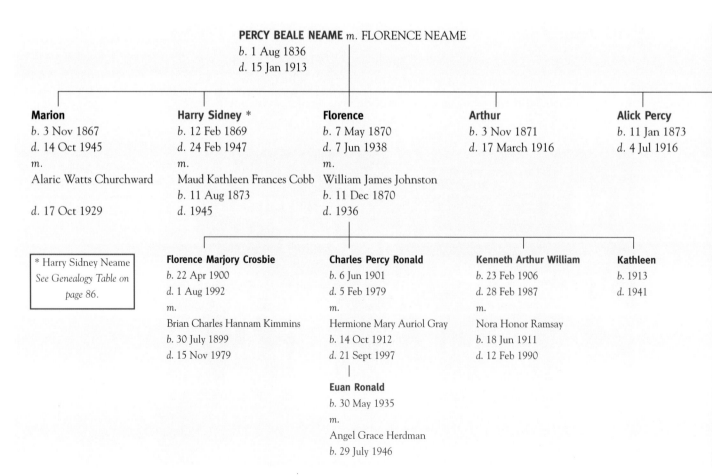

PERCY BEALE NEAME *m.* FLORENCE NEAME
b. 1 Aug 1836
d. 15 Jan 1913

Marion	**Harry Sidney ***	**Florence**	**Arthur**	**Alick Percy**
b. 3 Nov 1867	*b.* 12 Feb 1869	*b.* 7 May 1870	*b.* 3 Nov 1871	*b.* 11 Jan 1873
d. 14 Oct 1945	*d.* 24 Feb 1947	*d.* 7 Jun 1938	*d.* 17 March 1916	*d.* 4 Jul 1916
m.	*m.*	*m.*		
Alaric Watts Churchward	Maud Kathleen Frances Cobb	William James Johnston		
	b. 11 Aug 1873	*b.* 11 Dec 1870		
d. 17 Oct 1929	*d.* 1945	*d.* 1936		

> * Harry Sidney Neame
> *See Genealogy Table on*
> *page 86.*

Florence Marjory Crosbie	**Charles Percy Ronald**	**Kenneth Arthur William**	**Kathleen**
b. 22 Apr 1900	*b.* 6 Jun 1901	*b.* 23 Feb 1906	*b.* 1913
d. 1 Aug 1992	*d.* 5 Feb 1979	*d.* 28 Feb 1987	*d.* 1941
m.	*m.*	*m.*	
Brian Charles Hannam Kimmins	Hermione Mary Auriol Gray	Nora Honor Ramsay	
b. 30 July 1899	*b.* 14 Oct 1912	*b.* 18 Jun 1911	
d. 15 Nov 1979	*d.* 21 Sept 1997	*d.* 12 Feb 1990	

Euan Ronald
b. 30 May 1935
m.
Angel Grace Herdman
b. 29 July 1946

'quite worn out'. Grinding machinery in use since 1896 was also replaced by modern up-to-date plant. A 2½-ton petrol lorry was bought and a 5-ton steam lorry ordered, capable of doing much more work than the existing horse-drawn transport. After payment of dividends and directors' fees, nearly £12,000 remained to be carried forward.

The family suffered human losses, though not on active service. Arthur Neame, a prewar officer in the Faversham Volunteers, was recalled and took command of the Kent 2nd Heavy Battery stationed at Ightham near Sevenoaks. He was promoted to the rank of major; but he caught pneumonia and died at Ightham on 17 March 1916. His brother, Alick Neame, died at his home, Shirley House, London Road, Faversham, on 4 July of the same year, following an appendix operation.

While the sad loss of these two experienced family members, aged 44 and 43 respectively, did not affect the family's shareholding control, it lessened its share in the management and to that extent increased the Company's

Weathering the First World War

Charles Lawrence Graham,
Brewer 1880–1916, Director 1916–30.

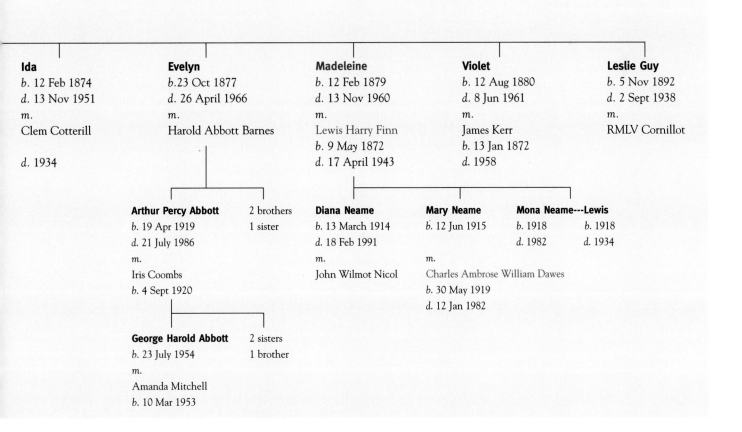

Ida	**Evelyn**	**Madeleine**	**Violet**	**Leslie Guy**
b. 12 Feb 1874	b. 23 Oct 1877	b. 12 Feb 1879	b. 12 Aug 1880	b. 5 Nov 1892
d. 13 Nov 1951	d. 26 April 1966	d. 13 Nov 1960	d. 8 Jun 1961	d. 2 Sept 1938
m.	m.	m.	m.	m.
Clem Cotterill	Harold Abbott Barnes	Lewis Harry Finn	James Kerr	RMLV Cornillot
		b. 9 May 1872	b. 13 Jan 1872	
d. 1934		d. 17 April 1943	d. 1958	

Arthur Percy Abbott   2 brothers
b. 19 Apr 1919   1 sister
d. 21 July 1986
m.
Iris Coombs
b. 4 Sept 1920

Diana Neame
b. 13 March 1914
d. 18 Feb 1991
m.
John Wilmot Nicol

Mary Neame
b. 12 Jun 1915
m.
Charles Ambrose William Dawes
b. 30 May 1919
d. 12 Jan 1982

Mona Neame---Lewis
b. 1918   b. 1918
d. 1982   d. 1934

George Harold Abbott   2 sisters
b. 23 July 1954   1 brother
m.
Amanda Mitchell
b. 10 Mar 1953

dependence on non-family board members. C.L. Graham, the head brewer, already a shareholder, was nominated on 15 June 1916 to the seat on the Board left vacant by Arthur Neame; and on the following 25 August G.E. Boorman, the company secretary, was nominated to that left by Alick Neame. Claude Wilkinson became assistant company secretary in December 1916 at a salary which was raised from £170 a year to £200 in June 1917; but by August 1918 he, too, was away on active service. Bonuses and pay increases were made in order to retain employees; and, having been informed at the second annual general meeting, in August 1916, that many tenants had been called up and that it was impossible to obtain new ones, the directors felt that 'in many cases' they would have to make reductions in rents.

A letter from Mason & Son, on 2 August 1916, to Shepherd Neame's chairman, reporting on the previous year's performance shows that the London auditor, having no doubt received the chairman's views on profit distribution, gave not only the usual accounting information but also helpful advice.

A Shepherd Neame 'steamer' on its way to Tankerton to collect fodder for the dray horses. Bystanders eagerly look on as engineers from the Brewery struggle to fix the main axle.

Dear Sir,

We have to report that we have now completed our investigation of the Accounts of your business for the year ending 30th June 1916.

The results of the trading are satisfactory, much more satisfactory indeed than we could have anticipated, the earnings after making all proper allowances being £29,537. 14s 6d compared with £32,756. 6s 1d for last year.

A substantial proportion of the profits of both years will have to be accounted for to the Government by way of Excess Profits Duty, but the balance which will remain is sufficient to justify the same dividend upon the Ordinary Share Capital as was paid last year, and to provide a substantial sum to be carried forward for equalisation of future dividends upon the Ordinary Shares.

After providing for Interest upon incumbrances and Debentures, for Dividend upon the Preference Shares, and for Directors' fees, there remains at your disposal the sum of £34,077. 6s 2d including the balance brought forward from last year.

Out of this sum you have paid £1,389. 9s 2d as interim Dividend upon the Ordinary Shares (less Income Tax), leaving £32,687. 17s 0d to be now dealt with.

For the purpose of meeting the claims which may be made against the Company for Excess Profits Duty, we recommend that the sum of £12,000 be carried to a Suspense Account and if this recommendation be acted upon, there will remain a balance of £20,687. 17s 0d.

After payment of a final dividend upon the Ordinary Shares of two and a half per cent together with a bonus of one shilling per Share (equivalent, with the Interim Dividend, to Ten per cent) there will remain to be carried to the next account £16,682. 19s 3d.

We are of the opinion that a final dividend at the above rate is fully justified by the results of the trading of the Year under review.

We cannot close this Report without recording our deep regret at the loss which the Company has sustained by the death of Major Arthur Neame and of Mr Alick Neame.

We are, Dear Sir,

Yours very faithfully,

(signed) Mason & Son

George Ernest Boorman, Company Secretary 1914–19, Director 1916–25. The appointment of Boorman and Graham to the Board marked a significant move by the Brewery to promote non-family members to directorial positions.

As the war progressed, not only were alcohol duties increased but the anti-drink section of the Liberal party made the most of any opportunity to limit drinking. Restrictions on opening hours, imposed by the government from April 1916 in order to save raw materials and to check any absenteeism which might result from loitering in pubs, had inevitable effects on Shepherd Neame's output. In the year ended 30 June, however, it was the Excess Profits Duty, as forecast by Mason, not these new restrictions, which concerned the second annual general meeting.

A year later, despite the new restrictions, earnings rose again, to £47,281, an increase far greater than price inflation. After £21,000 had been set aside

CHARACTERS

I t was agreed in April 1931 to present those staff who had completed 50 years service with a gold waistcoat pocket watch, at a cost of £12 each. After the Second World War gold wristlet watches were presented to long-serving staff.

Edwin Manning Edwards, who had joined Shepherd Neame in 1896 as an office boy when, as he recalled, only four

clerks were employed, and had risen to company secretary in 1919, was promoted to the Board in 1947. He received a gold wristlet watch in August 1946, having completed 50 years service on 10 August. His death, still in harness, was reported at the AGM in September 1955.

However, it was not just company directors who received awards for long service and dedication to the Company.

The people pictured below are just a very few of those whose names appeared in the 250th anniversary booklet in appreciation of the number of years they worked at the Brewery. The dates below their names show when they started work.

Such colourful characters have left their mark on Shepherd Neame, both by their personalities and their example of loyalty of service.

Gerald Adley Paice
Head Clerk, Yard Office, 1898

Claude Wilkinson
Cashier, 1899

Charles Field
Foreman, Bottling Department, 1907

Douglas William Cornfoot
Head Traveller, 1910

Harry Jarman Balls
Head Clerk, Wine and Spirit Dept., 1899

Edward George Longley
Brewer, 1900

Arthur Joseph Rogers
Foreman Carpenter, 1901

William Eustace Neame
Head Clerk, Bottling Department, 1906

When Jasper Neame, the chairman's elder son, married in 1933, his father gave a dinner to all staff and employees to mark the occasion.

for Excess Profits Duty, a dividend of 5 per cent was declared on the ordinary shares plus a bonus of 10 per cent, though the sum carried forward was cut to £27,702. Donations had been made to particular staff members in recognition of extra work 'caused by government restrictions' and a general distribution of £250 was made to the staff as a whole. Also, £75 a year was being paid to staff on active service in support of their dependants.

Satisfactory results continued to be reported during the last year of the war, earnings (with interest on savings in war bonds) going up to £55,437. Dividends were maintained and directors' fees raised from £1,370 to £1,400. A total of £400 was distributed among the staff, including those serving with the army.

Shepherd Neame Ltd had weathered the uncertainties of war well.

Edwin Manning Edwards,
Company Secretary 1919–47,
Director 1947–55.

The hurried return to peace

The boom after the First World War and the unregulated transition to peacetime operation posed new problems, though the lack of regulation meant that those in the services were able to return to Faversham without delay. G.E. Boorman took the opportunity to resign as company secretary on 6 February 1919 on the return of Edwin Manning Edwards who replaced him. Claude Wilkinson, after a very short time away, resumed his position as assistant company secretary. Payment of bonuses on 25 June 1919 – again for 'additional work entailed through government restrictions' – reveals the names of other loyal members of staff, including some of the recently recruited women, as well as returned ex-servicemen.

Secretary	£50	E. Wrigley	£25
R.F. Cook	£30	S.F. Brown	£15
H. Wilkinson	£30	A. Court	£10
E. Wilkinson	£30	Miss F.L. Bourke	£10
F. Howland	£30	T.E. Beer	£2 10s
P.A. Ellis	£30	Miss Minter	£2 10s
H.J. Balls	£30	Miss Bufford	£2 10s
G.A. Paice	£30	Miss Smith	£2 10s
D. Cornfoot	£25	E. Wraight	£2

Relationships between management and employees in the country as a whole changed during the war partly because of the effect of labour shortages and partly because of the better understanding of class differences arising from shared hardships and dangers. State pensions, introduced by Act of Parliament in 1908, began to be supplemented by company awards for long service. To that extent employees relied less on lifetime savings. At Shepherd Neame, for instance, J.E. Newport, who retired in May 1918, having served the Company for 47 years, was awarded £1 a week for the rest of his life.

The Whitley Committee on the Relations of Employers and Employees, in its first report published in July 1917, had proposed the formation of Joint Industrial Councils at national, district and works levels. This new climate was reflected at Shepherd Neame by the voting of £5,000 in August 1919 towards the creation of a Provident Fund for staff and employees, supplemented early in the following year by £6,000 in 5 per cent victory bonds. Harry Neame, C.L. Graham and G.E. Boorman became the Fund's first trustees.

The Company continued to make good profits, earnings with interest totalling £59,219 in the year 1918/9. It was agreed that the managing director's fee should be increased to £1,600 from 1 July 1918 with the use of Alfred House 'to be placed in suitable repair'. A bonus of £1,000 was to be shared among the other directors 'to be divided among them as they may think fit'.

An invitation that was turned down at this time deserves mention in the light of later ventures into catering. In April 1919 Shepherd Neame was invited to undertake catering on the Dover–Ostend ferries, and G.E. Boorman investigated this matter. The Board decided, however, that this was a 'class of business' which called for 'special knowledge and experience'. The invitation was declined because it 'could not be adequately dealt with to ensure satisfactory results'.

The postwar years saw an extension of the Brewery's fermenting plant in a new building abutting on the first floor workroom of Harry Child's adjoining haberdashery shop, with a window installed for ventilation. More motor vehicles were also purchased to cut distribution costs.

In the difficult deflationary year 1920/1 stocks were written down and profits fell but ordinary dividends were kept at 25 per cent because of sums carried

48

A story that's been brewing
for 300 years

This wall clock was presented to the Board in October 1923 by Mrs Churchward, the eldest of Percy Neame's daughters.

forward. The business continued to flourish. The contact between Reginald Mason and Harry Neame became closer. On 26 July 1922 the friendly auditor, then on holiday at the Old England Hotel, Windermere, wrote to the Shepherd Neame chairman. (It was still not customary to use Christian names.)

> Dear Neame,
>
> I have received a comparative statement of your profits. I congratulate you on the excellent result. I note that you propose to give them 25% and that your carry forward will be increased by about £19,000 after adding to the Provident Fund. This means leaving about 55% of the earnings undistributed and I gather that you have on your mind the new clause in the Finance Act 1922 about supertax on the undistributed profits of private companies.
>
> I don't think I would worry about this…I have little doubt that in your case we could avoid any interference. For one thing your business is largely assisted by loans and considerable capital is required for this. Again, for the large number of family interests it is particularly one which requires consolidating so that the income of the beneficiaries may be maintained at a regular figure…

The year 1921/2 had, in fact, been another most successful one. An ordinary dividend of 30 per cent, not the chairman's proposed 25 per cent, was declared.

In October 1923 Mrs Churchward, the eldest of Percy Neame's daughters, presented the Company with what the minutes describe as 'an antique English Wall Clock' for use in the boardroom, on behalf of herself and her five sisters.

They had good reason to celebrate the way that Shepherd Neame Ltd had managed to weather, surprisingly profitably, the transition to peacetime.

CHAPTER FOUR

The Twenties and Thirties

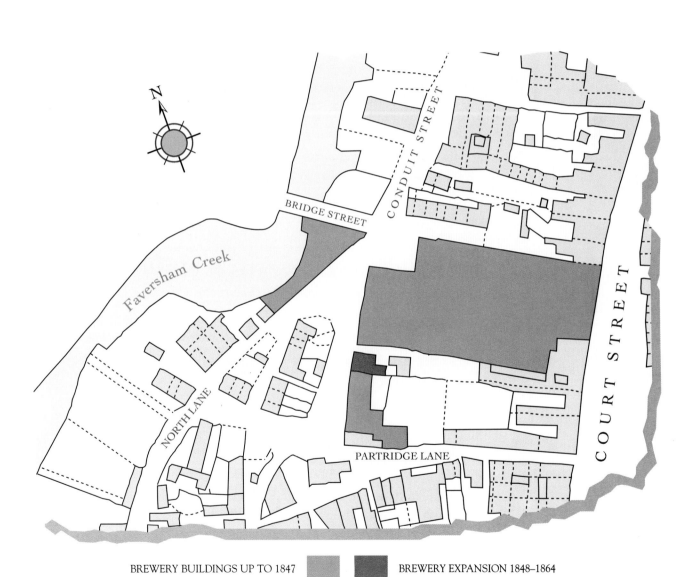

BREWERY BUILDINGS UP TO 1847   BREWERY EXPANSION 1848–1864

I F we look back on the interwar years in Britain as a whole, they are seen as a period of dislocation and difficulty. The early 1920s witnessed much labour conflict leading to the General Strike in 1926. This was very different from the United States, which enjoyed a great boom – the roaring twenties. But this ended in the Wall Street Crash of 1929, soon communicated to the rest of the world because America played a leading part in the international economy. By the beginning of 1931 world trade had fallen by a third in value. In the same year Europe, not least Britain, suffered from a financial crisis, government economies and rising unemployment. The numbers unemployed in Britain, which averaged 1.1 million in 1927, had grown to an average of 2.75 million in 1932 and were still up at 1.5 million in 1939.

Kent, however, together with the other home counties, fared better than the rest of the kingdom. Shepherd Neame Ltd, ably led by Harry Neame and supported on the Board from November 1925 by his elder son, Jasper Beale Neame (Jasper), and from April 1931 by his younger son, Laurence Beale Neame (Laurie), continued to do well. This is evident from both barrelage and earnings. (Barrelage before the war, 40,000 more or less in Edwardian years, had peaked at 45,447 in 1913.)

Trading through the Twenties

Public house outlets were hard to acquire. In June 1924, for instance, Shepherd Neame paid £4,000 for the freehold of the Coach and Horses, St Leonards on Sea, including furniture and fittings, for which the tenant was to pay rent of £50 a year. In October 1924, £2,650 was given at auction in Hastings for the Abbey Hotel, Battle. In March 1925, £2,000 was paid for the Unicorn and Prince of Wales at Bekesbourne and, in the following August, £3,600 to Canterbury Electric Theatre for the freehold of the Freemasons Tavern there.

Company performance, 1922/3–1931/2

Year ended June	Barrelage	Earnings (£) (Earnings plus interest on investment and loans)	
1922/3	62,123	48,209	(51,628)
1923/4	65,674	53,215	(57,627)
1924/5	65,476	50,670	(55,291)
1925/6	69,750	55,638	(60,687)
1926/7	70,645	60,372	(65,641)
1927/8	69,627	56,960	(62,362)
1928/9	68,357	58,284	(64,648)
1929/30	70,086	62,692	(69,584)
1930/1	67,970	62,649	(68,616)
1931/2	60,220	54,689	(61,249)

SOURCE Shepherd Neame Company Records

An account book listing sales to clubs shows that the Company made great efforts to develop this trade from 1921 onwards. (See Appendix A on p. 105.) Only 27 clubs had been supplied between 1906 or 1907 and 1911. Over 150 – in Kent, Essex, Surrey, Hampshire and parts of London – were supplied after 1921. Shepherd Neame often lent money in their support. Many were clubs of working men, often in heavy labouring jobs. Others were political in nature. There were some Old Comrades clubs in the early 1920s though they did not survive long – unlike the servicemen's clubs and those of police forces. Some were eccentricities, such as the (unlocated) Swimming and Dancing Club.

Regular payments continued to be made to the Provident Fund, loyal members retired after long service being given particular consideration. When G.E. Boorman left 'after 55 years faithful service' in August 1925 (as a Board member from 1916), he was awarded a pension of £480 per annum with the use of Richmond Cottage, Herne Bay, with all costs and outgoings for the rest of his life. A bathroom was immediately added to the premises at the further cost of £223. He died a few years later, and in August 1928 an annuity of £50 a year was purchased for his widow.

Boorman was a very special, non-family pensioner. As more members of staff and other employees completed 50 years service, it was agreed, in April 1931, to present each of them with a gold watch, purchased for about £12 each. H.J. Lucas, then serving at Camberwell Stores, received his gold watch, having retired on 18 March after 50 years service. It was then noted that John Luckhurst, formerly storekeeper at Sittingbourne, had completed his 50 years in July 1919 and had gone on working for the company until January 1924; and that J. Rogers, formerly wine and spirit storekeeper, had served for 50 years in October 1927 and continued to work until March 1930. They both received their gold watches in June 1931.

In the summer employees held what was known as their Annual Beanfeast. In June 1926 the Board, noting the increase in numbers attending (104), decided to make a contribution of £26 'towards the day's expenses'. In the following year 5s per head was allowed to all employees who were to go to the beanfeast on 25 June.

Thriving in the Thirties

In the 1930s those in employment benefited. Earnings fell less than prices, thanks to imports of cheaper food and raw materials. For Shepherd Neame, although output and company earnings were both below the 1920s totals, results were, as the auditors noted characteristically in one of their annual letters, such that 'the shareholders need have no cause for undue disappointment'. Economies in all branches of the business – apart from motor transport, the continued development of which was essential for the reduction of distribution costs – were announced at the annual general meeting in 1933, after a sharp fall in barrelage. The additional motor vehicles made it possible to supply Ashford and Canterbury from Faversham and to close the stores there.

The 'patriotic' nature of brewing – the fact that beer could be brewed entirely from home-grown materials – was brought up again at this time. Extra duties, imposed in 1931, were remitted in 1933 after

The requisitioning of horses by the War Department during the First World War necessitated the introduction of motor transport into the Brewery's everyday operations. The Thorneycroft delivery lorry was one of the vehicles in service for the Brewery during the 1930s.

Company performance, 1931/2–1938/9			
Year ended June	Barrelage	Earnings (£) (Earnings plus interest in investment and loans)	
1931/2	60,220	54,689	(61,249)
1932/3	57,938	54,438	(61,144)
1933/4	62,862	58,115	(64,650)
1934/5	65,678	59,638	(66,010)
		Profit	
1935/6	67,246	62,748	
1936/7	67,781	61,513	
1937/8	66,042	60,693	
1938/9	65,240	57,373	

SOURCE Shepherd Neame Company Records. From the year 1935/6 the method of reporting results was changed.

the Brewers' Society had submitted statistics from 85 per cent of the industry. 'It is of the greatest importance,' the Society urged, 'that all connected with the brewing industry should do their utmost to support the agricultural interest.'

In that year, 1933, Harry Neame was able to report that the company used only Kent hops and that 75 per cent of its malt was made from English barley. From 1925 most of the hops had, in fact, been bought from Lewis Finn who had married Madeleine, one of Percy Neame's six daughters, and farmed at Queen Court, Ospringe.

The 1930s saw a great increase in demand for bottled beer throughout the country. Unmechanised hand-bottling was no longer adequate. Shepherd Neame invested considerable sums in extending, updating and mechanising its bottled beer department. In 1937, when the chairman reported on how far this work had progressed, he also remarked upon the increased turnover of wines and spirits. Capital also continued to be invested in public houses, including the White Lion, Selling, bought in 1935 for £2,300.

Women and children worked together picking hops, as seen here in the mid-1930s.

Hop sacks being delivered to the Brewery in 1945.

Below and right: Ground malt ('grist') is mixed ('mashed') with hot water to make 'wort'. Hops are then boiled with the wort and it is later fermented to make beer. After the wort is run off, the spent grains are shovelled out of the mash tuns by hand and sent off for cattle feed.

Bill Wise at the wort coolers. The water used to cool the hot wort was warmed by the heat transfer and used in the next brew.

The White Lion, Selling, bought by Shepherd Neame in 1935 – one of the many pubs invested in by the Brewery in the 1930s.

Additions continued to be made to the Provident Fund and more long-serving stalwarts received their gold watches: Frank Beer after 51 years (since 1916 as a lorry driver) in 1933; Harry Wilkinson, head clerk, in 1934; and Albert Edward Eastman, storekeeper at Ashford, in 1937. The chairman himself completed his 50 years in 1938. He was presented with a blue leather-bound book with his initials, H.S.N., in gold on the front cover. Inside is a tribute inscribed in a copperplate hand. There then follow 239 names in alphabetical order, including those of 33 women. Although the business had become sizeable by then, one receives the distinct impression that the chairman – and perhaps others on the Board – rarely failed to recognise and acknowledge a very large proportion of the men and women employed.

Investment in the expanding business, Provident Fund contributions and other payments did not mean that the shareholders – mostly Neame family members and some senior executives – were not also well rewarded. Indeed, the dividends paid between the wars seem extraordinarily large until it is remembered that they were percentages of the nominal capital when the company was formed in 1913 and did not take account of the subsequent fall in the value of the pound or further investment. Even so, the dividends paid in the interwar years upon the wholly unreal nominal capital of pre-1914 are positively mouth watering: 45 per cent on debentures and ordinaries every year in

The Directors, Staff and Employees, past
and present, at the Faversham Brewery and
Stores, and at Alfred House, Faversham
unanimously offer their congratulations to

Mr Harry S Neame

who has been associated with the Brewery
for a period of fifty years, during twenty-five
of which he has so ably occupied the position
of Chairman and Managing Director of the
Company.

They ask his acceptance of this record
of the names of subscribers, and the accompanying
gift, as an expression of gratitude for the
kindness, and consideration Mr Neame has
shown to all who have worked with him in
the business that has prospered so greatly
under his control.

17ᵗʰ September 1938.

The tribute paid by his staff to Harry Neame in 1938.

the later 1920s, rising to 50 per cent between 1929/30 and 1933/4, and 55 per
cent between 1934/5 and 1937/8, during which time an additional 1 per cent
was added to the 5 per cent cumulative preference shares.

The directors engaged in management divided among themselves bonuses
rising from the £1,000 we saw them awarded in 1918 to £2,800 in 1935, while
Harry Neame, receiving £1,600 in 1918 as managing director, was paid £2,463
in 1935. He would receive a pension of £1,500 a year on his retirement, the

freehold of Alfred House having been sold to him by the Company for £1,500. Nor was that all. When Jasper Neame went to the School of Malting and Brewing at Birmingham University, the expense was borne not by his father but by the Company. There were other, smaller 'perks' which managing directors of a family company could award to themselves. They were just rewards – but only from such a prosperous and well-managed business.

Prosperity ensured not only the survival of the independent family business but also the better condition and prospects for everyone from the chairman to the latest recruit – and for Faversham as a town as well as for other places where Shepherd Neame traded.

Returned bottles being washed and inspected by Gladys Patchery before the Second World War.

CHAPTER FIVE

The Second World War

BREWERY BUILDINGS UP TO 1864   BREWERY EXPANSION 1865–1900

GERMANY invaded Poland on 1 September 1939, in response to which Britain and France declared war on Germany two days later. In mobilising men and resources, the British government bore in mind the lessons which had been learned during the war that had ended less than 21 years before. Conscription was not deferred; indeed the call-up of men aged 20 to 21 had been announced in the previous April after the German occupation of parts of Czechoslovakia the month before. Conscription for men between 19 and 41 was announced on 2 September, the day before Britain's declaration of war. Bacon, butter and sugar rationing followed early in January 1940. Beer, however, was not rationed.

This time indeed, every effort was made to increase beer production to satisfy social need and maintain morale while reducing the specific gravity in order to save resources. An advisory committee was formed to liaise with the

A British 'booze wagon'. The beer is being transferred from kegs to a modified fuel tank for delivery by an awaiting Spitfire to the RAF in Normandy.

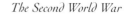

Dorothy Shuttle (left) and Elsie Clancey in the wine & spirit store using copper measures (see below) to fill jars. Dorothy Shuttle became forewoman during the Second World War when Charlie Derby, the foreman at the time, went into the RAF.

Ministry of Food on behalf of the brewing industry as a whole. Areas of supply were limited geographically so that each brewery could save on transport costs. Meanwhile, of course, excise duties were repeatedly raised to produce additional income for the war effort.

Harry Neame was already 70 years old when war broke out again. Shepherd Neame was lucky that his two sons, Jasper (born 1904) and Laurie (born 1908), still young enough to stand the pace yet experienced in management, were available to provide the all-important leadership in the business.

By 1940 75 people were already away in the forces. Others were recruited to take their place, women as well as men. Those who left included the head brewer, B.A. (Ben) Barnes, whose place was taken by his deputy E.G. (Ted)

Shepherd Neame directors and staff served in the Royal Observer Corps during the Second World War. Their job was to identify and observe aeroplanes all night and in all weathers.

Back row: C. Fuller, S.H. Dunn, C.S. Taylor, W. Capon, F. Gulliford, H. Ely, D.W. Harris, W.F. Taylor, E.P. Cutting, A.E. Bacon.

Front row: E.W. Coulter, R.G. Kempton, J.B. Neame, T.E. Beer, A.H. Carter.

Longley, assisted by Gordon Ely and his wife. Those with experience had the extra task of training and supervising the newcomers – and at the same time of serving in the Home Guard, or as special constables or fire watchers during the years when, from the Battle of Britain in 1940 onwards, Kent was in the front line. Others served in the Observer Corps, identifying and observing aeroplanes, all night and in all weathers. Dog fights took place overhead and enemy planes unloaded their bombs on Shepherd Neame properties both at that time, when enemy invasion was feared, and subsequently, when allied invasion forces were being assembled.

A list of properties damaged was reported to the Board. They included:

Sheerness Stores
Camberwell Stores
Two cottages at Penge
Chandos, Dover
Prince of Wales and Unicorn, Bekesbourne
Duke of Cumberland, Whitstable
George & Dragon, Canterbury
Property in bond at West India Docks

At the annual general meeting held on 21 August 1940, with the Battle of Britain nearing its peak and invasion still possible, the redoubtable Harry

Neame confessed that, as he was 'doing little work', he had decided to divide his commission among the active directors. He had handed over as managing director to Jasper Neame on 8 February 1940 'with general control of the business subject to such directions as shall from time to time be given him by the Board' and this was confirmed at the 1940 AGM. A year later the chairmanship was also passed to Jasper. Laurie Neame became vice-chairman and deputy managing director. Harry Neame himself remained on the Board, and at the 1942 AGM he proposed the vote of thanks to his two sons, a traditional courtesy. He spoke of the 'tremendous amount of attention' they had both paid to the business, resuming early morning duties and working every Saturday and Sunday throughout the year. This seems an astonishing claim but it must have been true, for the other Board members were well placed to judge. Though a splendid example *pour encourager les autres*, this was not a regime that could be maintained without interruption. Harry Neame noted in 1942 that his sons had not had a holiday for over two years, and the minutes were to record, in May 1943, that Laurie had just returned to the office after illness.

Jasper Beale Neame – Harry Sidney Neame's eldest son – Brewer 1925, Director 1925–41, Managing Director 1940–41, Chairman 1941–61. A busy committee man, Jasper Neame represented Kent on the council of the Brewers' Society, served on the Brewing Materials committee and its Hop Grading and Hop Costing sub-committees, and was a member of the Kent Brewers' Union, serving as its chairman and vice-chairman on several occasions. He was mayor of Faversham from 1946 to 1949 and became High Sheriff of Kent in 1954.

An opportunity declined

The Neame and Cobb families were related by Harry Neame's marriage to Maud Kathleen Frances Cobb, of the brewing family of Margate Cobbs. According to Shepherd Neame records, the Cobb brewing business then consisted of the Brewery at Margate, 40 licensed houses (39 freehold with off-licences), several private properties and two sites. The eccentric Francis Marsden Cobb had been warned against making a will (so it is said) by the palm-reading prophecies of a gipsy. When he died, intestate, the business was

Laurence Beale Neame – Jasper Beale
Neame's younger brother – Brewer 1931,
Director 1931–61, Managing Director
1961–1970. A Cambridge graduate (MA),
Laurie Neame was an athletics blue and
international quarter miler. He went on
to do the brewing course at Birmingham
University.

Harry Matthews fining barrels in the beer
store during the Second World War.

put up for sale. On 18 July 1941 the Shepherd Neame directors considered correspondence from Messrs Fleuret Haxell, Marks, Barley, giving particulars of the sale 'in pursuance of an Order of the High Court, Chancery Division' dealing with his estate. The minutes went on to note that the directors gave what is described as 'careful consideration' to the matter but in the end instructed the secretary to reply that 'under the present conditions they are not disposed to negotiate for the property'. No reason was given for this decision nor has any explanation been passed down over the last half century. In July 1941 Shepherd Neame had just completed a most successful trading year. Presumably the thinking was that it was prudent to remain satisfied with good results from the existing business rather than risk having to borrow money for such a large, sudden expansion, especially in the uncertainty of wartime. The sale was withdrawn and the Cobb business continued independently.

Harry Neame himself continued to take an interest in Brewery matters and in the social life of Faversham until his death on 24 February 1947. He had just celebrated his 78th birthday.

The Board minutes provide many insights into the problems which were so successfully overcome during these exacting years. There were, for instance, great difficulties in securing Shepherd Neame's quota of barley in 1941/2: in the end it was obtained before the end of the malting season 'although at a price higher than has ever been paid before…and some of the samples were very inferior'. The deteriorating state of the public houses was also a cause of concern. A special reserve fund was formed for repair and maintenance when this became possible.

Another reserve fund was established into which money was placed every time the excise duty on beer was raised. This was to take account of losses on stocks when and if the duty were to be reduced again. (Both these funds were shrewd means of offsetting some of the Company's large wartime taxation.) There were two duty increases in 1939/40, and more in 1940/1, 1941/2 and 1942/3. By 1943 Shepherd Neame's duty reserve stood at £35,000 and its repair and maintenance reserve at £8,000. In 1942/3 the Company paid as much as £481,000 in beer duty, £97,000 more than in the previous year.

E.M. Edwards, the company secretary, was particularly hard pressed because his deputy, M.N. Bartlett, went into the forces early in the war and became a squadron leader in the RAF. Contributions continued to be made to the staff and employees' superannuation and pension funds. In 1943 it was noted that £28,000 had been invested since the Provident Fund had been started. Dividends on the Company's nominal capital also remained considerable, though not so high as in prewar years: 25 per cent in 1939/40, less income tax at 8s 6d in the £; 35 per cent in 1940/1, less income tax of 10s in the £1; 40 per cent less tax in 1941/2 and 1942/43; 45 per cent less tax in 1943/4.

Lewis Harry Finn, Director 1925–43.

Family matters

As we saw in the previous chapter, the Company had bought most of its hops from Lewis Finn, who farmed at Queen Court, Ospringe. Having married into the family, he had become a director in 1925. When he died in 1943, Harry Neame spoke highly of him:

> He was always very thorough in the work he did and always gave us very sound advice. I do not think we ever adopted anything at the meetings that Mr Finn did not approve.

After his death the company took steps to acquire the freehold of Queen Court Farm and achieved this in October 1944, paying £33,000 for it, at the top of the range reached by Shepherd Neame's valuer, Charles Edgar. Jasper Neame told the Company:

Madeleine Finn, Director 1943–57.

> We purchased the Farm with the idea of ensuring a good supply of hops to our Brewery and as the prospect for the crop this year was favourable, we

Rowing to the rescue in Whitstable, 1953. Postwar flooding wrought more damage in many areas than wartime bombs, and Shepherd Neame did not escape the deluge...

The combination of high tides and high winds which flooded the north coast of Kent at the end of January 1953 caused Faversham Creek to overflow into the lower part of the Brewery. The need to take preventative measures against future flooding caused the Company to put in 60 ft piling when it came to build its new bottle store and a thick honey-combed concrete base on top of the piles.

The worst happened on the night of Saturday 31 January. According to the Board minutes, as soon as it was realised that the lower part of the Brewery and adjacent premises were to be under water, Laurie Neame rallied as many employees as he could to minimise the damage. Work went on non-stop from the Saturday night to 4.30 a.m. on Sunday and, after a break, until later that morning in order to get all the lorries into a fit state to make their Monday morning deliveries. 'The object was achieved,' the minutes report laconically. T.E. Beer and G. Hazelden were singled out for particular praise, the former being rewarded with a Parker 51 pen and the latter with a Rolls dry shaver.

Most of the licensed premises in Sheerness were still cut off some days later and known to have been damaged as were others in Whitstable and Herne Bay. The low-lying Sportsman at Seasalter suffered very badly; the licensee actually had to be rescued from the pub by rowing boat!

In 1944, a year after the death of Lewis Finn, Shepherd Neame acquired the freehold of Queen Court Farm in order to have a reliable supply of hops for the Brewery. Pictured here is one of the farm's hop fields, a familiar sight to all those pickers who used to travel down from London every summer for the beginning of the season.

hope to grow more hops than will be required for our own use. The hop position has not been at all good for these last few years and I feel that we are correct in ensuring a supply of hops to the Brewery.

Lewis Finn's nephew, Tom Finn, who already managed other properties, was engaged to manage Queen Court Farm for £600 per year. A separate farm account was opened so that its performance could be carefully monitored. Madeleine Finn was co-opted as a director after her husband's death and her appointment was confirmed at the subsequent AGM.

Unlike the Finns, who played a significant part in Shepherd Neame's history during the war, the Johnstons – Charles Percy Ronald (born 1901) and Kenneth Arthur William (born 1906), sons of another of Percy Neame's six daughters, Florence – were both away on war service, as their father had been during the First World War.

Kenneth Johnston's name appears frequently in the Board minutes. At the AGM in August 1940, when he was still only a second lieutenant at the Training Battalion, Welsh Guards, he wrote to say that his pay was only 17s 6d per day (just over £319 per year). Would the Board make it up? The Board agreed to pay him £800 a year less his army pay and allowances. At the same time it also supplemented the pay of other employees in the forces, larger sums being paid to those who had wives and children to support. Captain Johnston, as he soon became, kept on seeking leave of absence from Board meetings, and in September 1944, on becoming an acting major, with pay at 38s 6d per day (not far short of £800 a year), he asked the Board for further supplementation. His request was turned down.

More happily, at the 1944 AGM, Jasper Neame was able to report 'a record year in every respect' with 'the highest output on record' (to be explained to some extent by 'the presence of British and allied forces stationed in our district'), and he went on to reflect upon the debt he owed his brother 'who has borne with me the anxieties of the business over these very troubled times'.

To have increased barrelage during these difficult wartime years with a reduced labour force was a great achievement. The upward revision of staff annual salaries in June 1941 enables us to list staff members who

Kenneth Arthur William Johnston,
Apprentice Brewer 1928, Director 1929–85,
Chairman 1961–71

Year ended March	UK barrels	Shepherd Neame annual barrels	Average specific gravity	Shepherd Neame profit (£)	
				Trading	Net (after deducting directors' fees and dividends)
1937/8	24,206,000	66,042	1,041.0	60,693	30,375
1938/9	24,675,000	65,240	1,040.9	57,373	27,003
1939/40	25,367,000	64,441	1,040.6	49,901	25,132
1940/1	26,204,000	66,516	1,038.5	73,330	26,934
1941/2	29,861,000	72,871	1,035.5	64,353	27,832
1942/3	29,297,000	69,836	1,034.3	66,273	29,291
1943/4	30,478,000	78,260	1,034.6	95,718	35,430
1944/5	31,333,000	82,507	1,034.5	87,986	32,531

United Kingdom and Shepherd Neame annual barrel production, the average specific gravity, and Shepherd Neame profit 1937/8 to 1944/5

SOURCES Brewers and Licensed Retailers Association, *Statistical Handbook;*
Shepherd Neame Company Records

helped to make possible the Company's remarkable performance at that critical time:

E.M. Edwards, company secretary since 1919	£800
C. Wilkinson, cashier	£400
H.B. Hills, accountant	£350
D.W. Cornfoot, head traveller	£336
E.G. Longley, assistant brewer	£324
H.J. Balls, chief clerk, wine and spirit department	£300
W.E. Neame, chief clerk, B B department	£300
E.W. Coulter, head clerk	£300
C.J. Pepper, third traveller	£251
T.E. Beer, second clerk, yard office	£250
A.F. Forster, second clerk, wine and spirit department	£250
E.G. Wraight, second clerk, B B department	£250
A.D. Ellis, ledger and counter clerk	£212
A.H. Forster, third clerk	£200
G.C. Ely, second assistant brewer	£164 plus house in Court Street
A.J. Beer, clerk, cash registry	£150

Customers enjoying a glass of beer.

That there are surnames repeated in this list, is a reminder that the family nature of Shepherd Neame extended beyond the Board. And, as with the Board, these ties were extended through marriage. All this applied to non-staff employees as well. Those who recall the particular loyalty of the wartime years, to which these family ties contributed, also remember that the occasional glass of beer helped, too!

Despite increased barrelage and good trading results, however, labour shortages grew worse as the war continued. The chairman reported in August 1945 'the worst year we have had for labour'. Even Italian prisoners of war were brought in to assist in the malthouse. The difficulties of the coming peace – especially full employment and wage inflation – were being foreshadowed.

CHAPTER SIX

The Challenge of Change

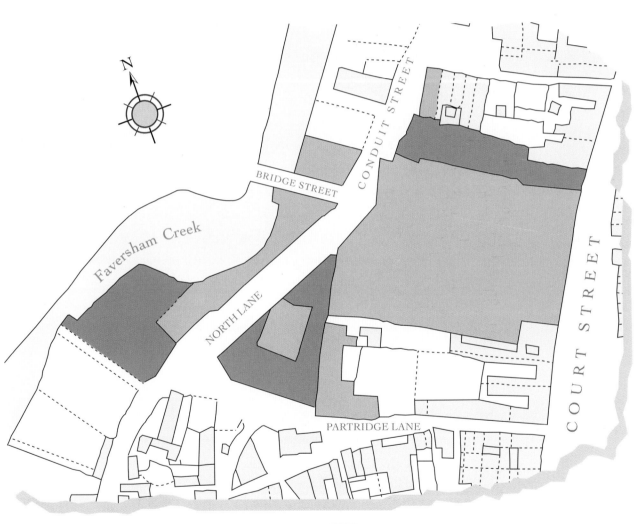

BREWERY BUILDINGS UP TO 1900 BREWERY EXPANSION 1901–1930

THE total number of brewery companies in the United Kingdom fell from 428 in 1940 (owning 840 breweries) to 362 in 1950 (owning 567). The brewery across the road from Shepherd Neame, which had become George Beer & Rigden in 1922 after W.E. and J. Rigden had amalgamated with Beer's Star Brewery in Canterbury, was taken over by Fremlins of Maidstone in 1948. How Shepherd Neame remained successful enough to retain its independence, and was eventually to emerge as the last Kent-based brewing firm to do so, is a tale of triumph over all the odds.

In 1945, Shepherd Neame was confronted with an exhausted labour force, declining sales and an estate in need of a great deal of investment. The dilemma was how to balance the expenditure between investment in plant and the need to modernise and raise the profile of the estate.

In the immediate postwar period Britain was a nation short of materials and money. Once the initial euphoria of victory had worn off, the end of the 1940s proved a difficult time as people struggled to rebuild their lives and homes; years of rationing and controls still lay ahead.

Postwar blues   During the war the only improvement at the Brewery allowed by the Ministry of Supply occurred in 1942 when permission was granted for the installation of a new cooling plant for yeast. Otherwise the reduced labour force was expected to provide much more beer from the existing plant by one means or another, and the same conditions prevailed for some years after the war. Peace was allowed to break out only slowly.

In 1945/6 production, at 83,603 barrels, exceeded the previous year's record by over 1,000 barrels; but the August 1946 AGM was told of the government's instructions to reduce output and gravity, and customers were restricted to a proportion of their previous year's purchases.

Labour problems persisted throughout the 1940s, and the only plant improvement was an electric generator installed to keep the beer-bottling and cask-washing plants in operation. At the 1947 AGM the chairman reported: 'It has certainly been the hardest year I can remember.' There had been power cuts. 'At one time in last year we were only able to brew *half* the quantity we required.'

Despite these hardships, profits continued at an average of 55 per cent during the period. At the same time, the alcohol strength of the beer was increased by 3 per cent. Output fell during the latter years of the 1940s, down 29,979 from the 1945/6 high to 53,624 in 1950/1. It was claimed, no doubt justly, that the fall in output was less than elsewhere in the county because of careful planning and savings. In March 1951 Shepherd Neame ceased to brew beer to retail at 11d a pint, a price that had been held for a considerable time, and raised it to 1s.

New legislation in 1948 had obliged Shepherd Neame, along with other companies, to publish more financial information about itself. Its growing reserves, then revealed, made it particularly attractive to predators. At the same time, death duties loomed ominously ahead with the possible need for the family shareholders to raise cash to pay them. The decision was therefore taken in 1951 to capitalise £212,493 into 210,000 non-voting 'A' shares which could be sold by family shareholders on a matched bargain basis without endangering the Company's independence.

At an extraordinary general meeting, held immediately after the AGM on 12 September 1951, Jasper and Laurie Neame were appointed joint managing directors for 10 years at salaries of £2,250 and £2,150 per annum respectively. Kenneth Johnston, who felt aggrieved at having fallen behind during his years away at war while others, in reserved occupations, had benefited, was appointed manager of the wine and spirit department for 10 years at a salary of £1,950.

Despite postwar transport difficulties, the enterprising licensee of the Vine, Tenterden, made hand-cart deliveries from his off-licence to his thirsty customers, until the 1950s.

Drive to increase
outlets

Shepherd Neame had already realised the need to acquire many more tied outlets for its products: it had purchased the Sportsman at Seasalter in 1947 and the freehold of the Marine Hotel, Tankerton, in 1949. The value of Shepherd Neame's freehold properties had increased from £420,000 to £461,000 in these two years, which put the Company's nominal capital of a mere £380,000 into its true context.

In September 1952 C.E.J. Rogers of Rogers, Son and Stevens was asked to act for the Company in acquiring 22 freehold licensed premises in Kent, Surrey and Sussex for a sum not exceeding £150,000 – a large leap forward. When this was turned down, a higher bid was authorised but also rejected. At this point Rogers was told to bid for certain of these properties when Nalder Collier Brewery & Investment Trust Ltd put them up for auction in London. Five houses were purchased for £39,200.

Shepherd Neame continued to buy prudently and purchased the Dog and Duck in Margate complete with all fixtures for £32,500 in April 1953. A new lease was taken on the George at Leeds from Lady Baillie's estate in the same year.

A considerable number of Kent pubs were bombed in the war and the government set up licensing planning areas covering the main towns where losses had occurred. New licences were allocated to Kent brewers on a proportionate basis to those lost due to war damage.

Shepherd Neame recognised the importance of increasing its number of licences if it was to strengthen its financial independence. As new licences were rarely granted, expansion came about through the purchases of existing businesses. In the mid-1950s, Courage made a tentative enquiry as to whether Shepherd Neame would be interested in selling its houses. However, the Brewery had no intention of doing so. Instead the policy of expansion continued and, at an extraordinary general meeting on 29 March 1956, it was agreed that the Waterside Brewery should be acquired from E. Mason & Co., the Maidstone brewers, together with 50 licensed premises and 8 off-licences. Arrangements were made to fund the purchase on 12 April 1956 by issuing £420,000 6 per cent debenture stock 1972–82 by trust deed to General Accident Fire and Life Insurance Corporation.

The arrangement was a good one, as the chairman told the shareholders:

> None of their houses is in competition with any of our existing houses and
> they are all situated away from coastal areas and not subject to such sea-
> sonal variations in the trade as we suffer with many of our houses in coastal
> towns. A number of Mason's houses are in and around Maidstone where we
> have not hitherto been represented. Practically the whole of Mason's trade
> is tied whereas in our case a large proportion is free, and this factor alone
> would greatly strengthen our position…[It is] an excellent opportunity for
> broadening and strengthening our business…it should result in important
> long-term advantages.

Brewing ceased in Maidstone and was concentrated in Faversham. Even
after this large acquisition, Shepherd Neame continued to buy further outlets
individually as suitable opportunities arose.

There was now a growing realisation amongst the brewing industry that
the public house was their main business asset. Charles Clore, the property
magnate, sharpened this awareness when he made an unsuccessful bid for
Watney Mann in 1959. Clore recognised that, in a number of instances, public house property was undervalued in respect of its alternative use. His bid sent
a clear warning to the brewing industry to review the value of their premises
more carefully and to make provision against similar takeover attempts. It also
initiated the start of a series of takeovers or amalgamations during the 1960s.
Shepherd Neame and other independent brewers had to take serious notice of
this threat if they were to survive in the long term, and the Board set about a
major improvement programme to make its pubs more attractive.

The emphasis throughout the war and just after had been to meet the
demand for beer. The conditions in which customers drank the beer were not
considered so important. Pubs were still very much a male preserve and, if a
house wanted to improve its seating in the saloon, an old bus seat was as
likely to be pressed into use as anything else.

As the war receded, however, people looked for improved facilities and for
a broader range of entertainment. This was initially reflected in the Workmen's

Wooden fermenters lined with copper. These were replaced with cylindro-conical stainless steel fermenting vessels in 1972.

During installation in 1972, one of the first two stainless steel fermenters became lodged in the timber roof. The vessel was finally set in its place when a carpenter freed it by carving away one of the beams.

In 1985, a batch of seven 480 barrel fermenters were installed, greatly increasing capacity and enabling the Brewery to meet continuing growth in the demand for lager.

This fermenter was one of a batch of four installed in 1995, giving an additional 2,000 barrel fermenting capacity. These were the first outdoor vessels.

After the Second World War, pubs were largely the preserve of working men seeking a drink and a chat. During the 1950s, 1960s and 1970s, however, pubs were developed to incorporate more entertainment and a wider range of products.

The bar at the Coach and Horses. Today's pub offers food as well as drink. Limited licensing hours and spartan interiors have become a thing of the past.

Clubs, which were important social centres for heavy industry and, increasingly, not only provided a place where working men could have a drink, but where the family could also have an evening out with bingo and live entertainment. At the same time, there was a growing demand from the local authorities for improvements to be carried out in houses, mainly relating to improvement in toilet and catering facilities.

At the start of the 1960s a further social change was taking place with the increased ownership and use of the motor car. At the AGM in 1962 the chairman's report expressed what was then up-to-date thinking about the pubs now that more customers drove there in their cars:

For this type of trade not only must the outside of the house look attractive but also *the inside must be comfortable and, if possible, such amenities as snacks and even meals must be available.*

Despite the arrival of the breathalyser in 1967, this trend continued and pubs were made more attractive by the development of food and restaurant facilities. Special catering courses were arranged for tenants in collaboration with Thanet Technical College, which specialised in the subject. Shepherd Neame's policy was more than justified when, in 1969, A.L. Weigh and his wife, of the White Lion, Selling, a small country pub specialising in good pub food, won the *Evening Standard* Pub of the Year Award out of 13,000 houses. Soon after that the Company began building car parks at all country pubs wherever possible.

The significance of bottling

A particular feature of the postwar years was a continued demand for bottled beers, which ensured a consistent product and gave the Company the opportunity of opening new free trade accounts outside its normal trading area.

Charlie, last of the Shepherd Neame dray horses and not averse to the occasional mouthful of beer himself. Plans to extend the site of the brewery to include new automatic line bottling equipment went ahead in the 1960s shortly after Charlie died: the end of horse-drawn transport, though fondly missed, finally released space to expand the bottling store and warehouse.

80

A story that's been brewing
for 300 years

The bottling plant in the new bottling
hall signalled increases in line-speed and
automation.

There was more profit to be made out of bottled beers than draught beer. However, bottling required considerable fixed capital outlay in respect of plant and increased warehousing facilities.

The Company had, in the late 1930s, invested considerable sums in replacing hand-bottling by a simple form of machine-filling. By 1959 bottling took nearly 30 per cent of Shepherd Neame's output. The replacement of the 21-year-old plant became imperative. In the week before the August bank holiday it was bottling just short of 500 barrels though the plant had been designed to handle 350 at most. Laurie Neame, the director responsible, warned the Board that a major breakdown of either of the two machines in mid-summer would be 'a disaster'. It was also noted at the time that spares were no longer made for this outdated equipment.

The subsequent expansion, which included new conditioning and bright beer tanks, bottling plant and new filters, was not completed until 1967. This led to significant developments, as at last the Company had spare capacity.

During the 1960s, Shepherd Neame had recognised that the public taste for beer was rapidly changing and the growth in lager was becoming a major part of the product range that had to be offered. In June 1968 Shepherd Neame agreed with Carlsberg Distribution Ltd to bottle Carlsberg lager for five years. In the same year, there was an additional benefit when Hürlimann lager was introduced with the guaranteed sale of 400 barrels to the Grasshopper at Westerham, which Hürlimann had recently purchased. This arrangement led to an amicable and lasting alliance between the two companies and enabled Shepherd Neame to export Abbey Ale to the 2,500 customers served by Hürlimann, mainly in the Zurich area in Switzerland.

Keg beer

It was in 1959 that Shepherd Neame first noticed that competition from the introduction of keg beer was damaging the Company's free trade sales. The Board decided that it should experiment with its introduction, despite the risk of being one of the first brewers to do so and recognising that, if it were successful, considerable capital investment would be required. The chairman's son, Robert Harry Beale Neame (Bobby), was allocated just £1,000 to set up plant and buy kegs for this purpose. He purchased two 20-barrel tanks from Mr Roberts of Tottenham, negotiating the deal in a Steptoe & Son type yard at the back of Tottenham Hotspur Football Club and sealing it with a meal of greasy lamb chops on a tablecloth of old newspaper.

Despite initial problems of quality control – pasteurisation was achieved by lowering the kegs in and out of two zinc baths, a Heath Robinson arrangement that produced variable results – the new keg beer proved popular, especially with young drinkers. It was marketed originally under the trade name Top Hat, and the trade was developed through a selected number of pubs. Although there had been a perceived threat to bottled beer, this did not materialise and the demand was such that in 1976 the company installed an automatic keg washing and racking machine.

Farming's variable profitability

The investment in farming, however, proved less successful. Queen Court had been acquired to make sure of a reliable supply of hops, and with the hope that it could be turned to profit by selling the surplus in good years. This was all very well when harvests were good; but it was a different story when losses were sustained. Farming was for farmers, not brewers. Shepherd Neame in fact increased its risks when, after a good farming year at Queen Court, it decided to buy Twitham Court Farm at Ash. There then followed a series of poor years between 1955 and 1958, although Shepherd Neame was one of the first to order a hop-picking machine, taking the decision to do so because labour was hard to find. Despite initial teething troubles, the machines proved their worth.

In September 1959, Bobby's younger brother Arthur Rex Beale Neame (Rex) took over from Bill Finn, who had managed the farms following the death of his father, Tom. However, the farm began to make a loss in the early 1960s and the situation did not improve even after Geoffrey Finn (a cousin of Tom) was called in as farming consultant. Rex Neame was told that his contract

Arthur Rex Beale Neame (Rex), Jasper Neame's second son, managed Queen Court Farm from 1959 to 1967, a period when labour was hard to find. He was elected to the Board in September 1961.

would not be renewed after September 1966. In December 1967 he took up an appointment with Bulmers as Orchard Development Manager to ensure that there would be a long-term supply of bittersweet apples for cider making.

Sole survivor

By cutting costs, on the one hand, and concentrating upon more profitable sales, on the other, Shepherd Neame had remained a most successful business. Net profit, which never exceeded £60,000 a year before 1961/2, rose sharply to £93,000 in 1964/5 and, after some fluctuation, exceeded £100,000 in 1971/2. The estimated value of freehold and leasehold properties also continued to rise and was reported to be in excess of £1,000,000 in 1955/6.

These good results were accompanied by much family tension. Jasper Neame and his younger brother, Laurie, had worked like Trojans together during the war with Jasper, the elder, becoming managing director (1940) and

Queen Court Farm, as it looks today. To help overcome the labour shortages of the late 1950s Shepherd Neame took the lead in acquiring a hop-picking machine.

chairman (1941), Laurie serving as his deputy in both instances. In the post-war era, a number of factors came together which changed the tenor of the industry and which had to be dealt with if the firm was to survive as an independent concern.

There had always been tension between the marketing side of the business and production, both competing for the available financial resources, but in the postwar conditions of the 1950s the trade and marketing side became an essential ingredient for success. In consequence, Jasper had become heavily involved with brewing trade politics, which took him away from Faversham for a considerable amount of time, leaving Laurie to struggle with day-to-day matters.

In the 1960s, the next generation grappled with the same difficulties. Jasper's elder son, Bobby Neame, came to work at the Brewery in 1956. He became a director in September 1957 when Madeleine Finn, who was due to retire by rotation, decided not to seek re-election. His father was ill at that time but was back at work in the following January. By the AGM in September 1959 Bobby Neame had considerably widened his range, being said to be 'helping in the Brewery and in charge of the free trade, advertising etc.'.

Laurie's son, Colin Roger Beale Neame, joined the company in October 1959 to help his father in the bottled beer department, a month later than Rex Neame who had joined to manage Queen Court. A year later he started to attend Board meetings with Rex, both as probationers, with the intention of their becoming full members in the following year. At the AGM in September 1961, their election was confirmed as full members.

Jasper Neame died on 18 January 1961 at the early age of 56. Laurie Neame then became sole managing director. He survived his brother for another nine years and he continued his interest in production. Kenneth Johnston succeeded Jasper as chairman, and the Board continued to ponder how best to invest for the future and to cater for consumer expectations.

Bobby had followed in his father's footsteps in taking particular interest in the sales side of the business. This became an especially important area as the larger brewers, better accustomed to advertising – including advertising on the new commercial television – came to compete in Shepherd Neame's sales area,

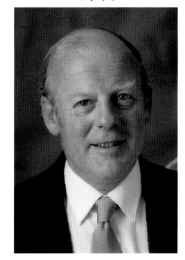

Colin Roger Beale Neame, Laurie Neame's eldest son, was recruited to help his father in the bottled beer department in October 1959. He was elected to the Board in September 1961. Colin was appointed production director on 1 July 1967.

*A story that's been brewing
for 300 years*

Right and below, a selection of beermats
and labels.

especially in the free, on-trade. It was agreed that from 1 July 1967 Bobby Neame should become marketing director 'with the special task of improving the image of the Company in the eyes of the public'; and the public relations firm of Good Relations Ltd, Canterbury were appointed 'to bring our name into more prominence with all classes of people in our trading area and to expand this area if possible'. Greater attention was paid to publicity, with advertising on Southern Television in 1970.

Colin took a keen interest in the technical, brewing side of the business which was in the ascendant during the 1960s and was equally important in fending off competition. He played a major part in the building of the new

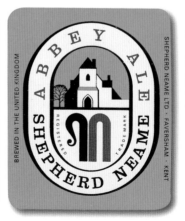

bottling plant, the introduction of keg beer and various improvements at the Brewery. At the same time that Bobby was appointed marketing director, Colin Neame was appointed production director. 'It will be his responsibility, working in conjunction with the head brewer and brewing staff, to see that the best possible beer is produced in the most economical way.' The chairman felt, justly, that Colin's and Bobby's appointments would benefit the company considerably and, rather optimistically, hoped that 'although they are complementary to each other, they will not in any way overlap'.

However, the underlying competition for funds between the two parts of the business continued. The tension was evident; but the business as a whole benefited. Both young directors were fighting their equally important corners. At the AGM in September 1970 it was recorded, very justly, that, as older directors retired, 'the company was most fortunate in having two such able directors of the next generation to carry on'.

After Colin Neame had been made production director, it was recorded that 'there has been a considerable transformation in the Brewery and many labour saving ideas had been introduced'. He was also responsible, in 1969, for the introduction of a small biochemical laboratory and employing a laboratory technician.

Every effort was made to save labour throughout the Company. 'Wages have now reached a level at which it is essential to install labour saving devices,' the Board reported in October 1966. Work study was introduced and

so were accounting machines. By October 1968 the labour force was down to 206. Shepherd Neame's financial policy remained very conservative, however, with the emphasis on cutting costs, ploughing back profits and reducing debt rather than borrowing money on advantageous terms to enable the business to grow more rapidly.

In the great economy drive Colin Neame took an interest in possible savings on transport from the Brewery. After having raised the matter without positive result, in May 1968 he drew the Board's attention to a report he had

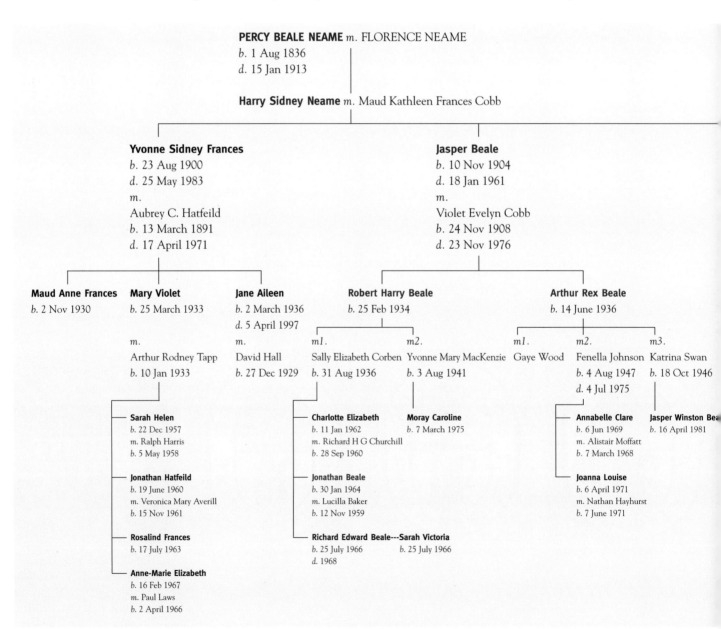

PERCY BEALE NEAME *m.* FLORENCE NEAME
b. 1 Aug 1836
d. 15 Jan 1913

Harry Sidney Neame *m.* Maud Kathleen Frances Cobb

Yvonne Sidney Frances
b. 23 Aug 1900
d. 25 May 1983
m.
Aubrey C. Hatfeild
b. 13 March 1891
d. 17 April 1971

Jasper Beale
b. 10 Nov 1904
d. 18 Jan 1961
m.
Violet Evelyn Cobb
b. 24 Nov 1908
d. 23 Nov 1976

Maud Anne Frances
b. 2 Nov 1930

Mary Violet
b. 25 March 1933
m.
Arthur Rodney Tapp
b. 10 Jan 1933

Jane Aileen
b. 2 March 1936
d. 5 April 1997
m.
David Hall
b. 27 Dec 1929

Robert Harry Beale
b. 25 Feb 1934

m1.
Sally Elizabeth Corben
b. 31 Aug 1936

m2.
Yvonne Mary MacKenzie
b. 3 Aug 1941

Arthur Rex Beale
b. 14 June 1936

m1.
Gaye Wood

m2.
Fenella Johnson
b. 4 Aug 1947
d. 4 Jul 1975

m3.
Katrina Swan
b. 18 Oct 1946

Sarah Helen
b. 22 Dec 1957
m. Ralph Harris
b. 5 May 1958

Jonathan Hatfeild
b. 19 June 1960
m. Veronica Mary Averill
b. 15 Nov 1961

Rosalind Frances
b. 17 July 1963

Anne-Marie Elizabeth
b. 16 Feb 1967
m. Paul Laws
b. 2 April 1966

Charlotte Elizabeth
b. 11 Jan 1962
m. Richard H G Churchill
b. 28 Sep 1960

Jonathan Beale
b. 30 Jan 1964
m. Lucilla Baker
b. 12 Nov 1959

Richard Edward Beale---Sarah Victoria
b. 25 July 1966   *b.* 25 July 1966
d. 1968

Moray Caroline
b. 7 March 1975

Annabelle Clare
b. 6 Jun 1969
m. Alistair Moffatt
b. 7 March 1968

Joanna Louise
b. 6 April 1971
m. Nathan Hayhurst
b. 7 June 1971

Jasper Winston Bea
b. 16 April 1981

received from G.J. Dungate, a work study specialist, explaining how the Company could save, he believed, £15,000 a year on loading, transport and direct delivery from Brewery to customer. After evidence of success over a two-year period, Dungate was appointed on a retainer basis and the arrangement remained in place until he retired.

It was in 1968 that the Cobb brewing company in Margate, which Shepherd Neame had decided not to buy in 1941 despite the family connection, again came on the market, together with 38 licensed premises. It had

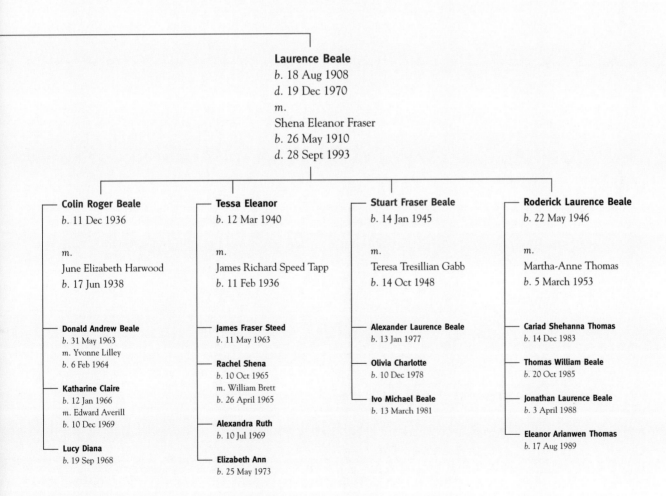

become increasingly difficult for the Cobbs to survive independently as the seaside trade on which its pubs had so relied was increasingly drawn to the Butlins hotels. It was taken over by Whitbreads in January 1968 and ceased to brew in the following October. As a result of this purchase, the Shepherd Neame minutes succinctly recorded on 25 October: 'We are the last independent brewery in Kent.'

CHAPTER SEVEN

Kent's Sole Surviving Brewery

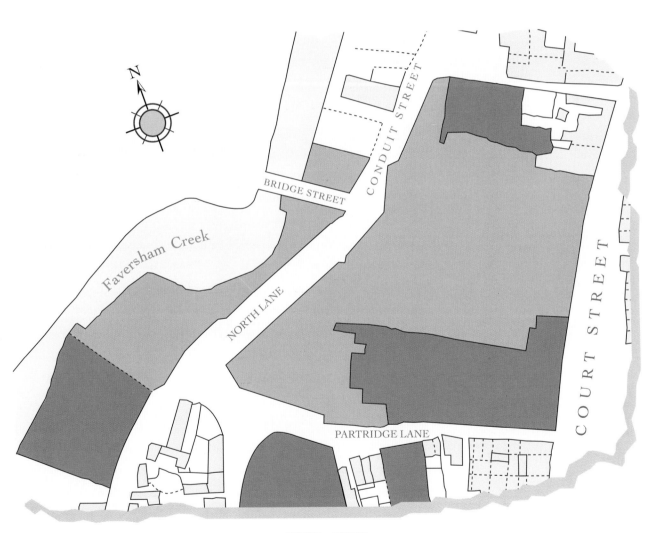

BRIDGE STREET

Faversham Creek

CONDUIT STREET

NORTH LANE

COURT STREET

PARTRIDGE LANE

BREWERY BUILDINGS UP TO 1930 BREWERY EXPANSION 1931 to date

THE matter of the future chairmanship had come up at the beginning of 1969. Laurie Neame, a firm advocate of division between chairman and managing director, had then advised that, since Bobby Neame had worked in the Company for considerably longer than Colin Neame, he should have the chairmanship if he wanted it, leaving Colin as managing director. Bobby did not favour this approach as he felt the Company could not work on a basis that did not integrate beer production and distribution sales to free trade and tied estate. Laurie died suddenly and unexpectedly at the end of the day on 19 December 1970 after all the excitement when his second son, Stuart, was married. Finally, when Kenneth Johnston was about to retire at the end of March 1971, he proposed that Bobby should become chairman and Colin managing director and vice-chairman, which was unanimously agreed.

In the early 1970s Ted Coulter decided to step down as company secretary. His subsequent retirement from the Board, 11 years later, marked the end of a career which spanned 61 years with Shepherd Neame, and the end of a management era in which a boy whose first task was cleaning shoes could aspire to climb to the top in a relatively small family business, and when chairman Harry Neame, grandfather of Bobby, could offer a miscreant facing dismissal the alternative of donating his wages for three weeks to the town's cottage hospital.

Ted Coulter would also remember many colourful characters, including the Brewery's betting fanatic who seemed always to be short of money. He would regularly approach Jasper Neame, pleading for an advance on his wages. When asked what the money was for, he would reply: 'It's like this, guv'nor. I haven't got any money to live on for the rest of the week because, as you know, you've got to speculate to accumulate.' There is no doubt that the slow horses showed him no mercy.

Further change at the top

Stuart Fraser Beale Neame, who had joined his brother Colin and cousin Bobby in 1972, after half a decade with IBM, took over as company secretary the following year. As if to highlight the changing style of management, Stuart had proposed the acquisition of a sophisticated IBM System 3 computer, despite the fact he had been warned before joining that the Board would be unlikely to invest in computers. He won the day and went on to design a number of innovative programs for telesales and distribution. News of Stuart's ingenuity and the success of his programs created considerable interest from other independent breweries, a number of which bought the software to improve their own systems. After four years with the Company, Stuart was co-opted on to the Board.

In the family, concern was being expressed that the shareholders were becoming spread through third and fourth generations and the directors moved to review the Company share structure. As the 5 per cent preference shares had equal voting rights with the B ordinary shares, it was decided to replace the preference shares with B ordinary shares and to enhance the voting rights of the B shares, which could be transferred only to the descendants of Percy Neame. At the same time the £1 A ordinary shares were given voting rights and a market was made introducing outside shareholders, based on an agreed price between a willing buyer and a willing seller.

While overall control was assured, another long-term problem at the top came to a head. The Board had become concerned that worsening tensions between vice-chairman Colin Neame and other members could threaten the future success of the Company. After 25 years service Colin left Shepherd Neame and resigned his directorship in 1984 to pursue other interests. In the following months, the Company also lost the services of Ted Coulter and Kenneth Johnston to retirement. The loss of so much experience in such a short time put more pressures on the chairman and the company secretary; so the Board accelerated plans to strengthen the management team by creating a Technical Board, heralding a cultural shift from home-grown talent to the drafting in of outside expertise. With the continued expansion of the Company, Bobby reduced his considerable outside responsibilities, resigning from the

Edward William (Ted) Coulter, Director 1961–84. Ted Coulter joined Shepherd Neame as a junior cleaning shoes and worked his way up to Director, retiring after 61 years with the Company.

**Jonathan Neame – Bobby Neame's son –
who was appointed a director in 1993.**

leadership of Kent County Council, and Stuart handed over his duties as company secretary in order to take on the role of vice-chairman.

The creation of a Technical Board proved to be the greatest single reorganisation in the Company's history. Previously, all decisions had been made by a main Board dominated by family members, thereby ensuring control of both the day-to-day running of the Company and its future. But the Brewery was expanding all the time and the need for wider professional direction had become paramount. The Technical Board, with the appointment of directors for finance, brewing, managed house, property/tenanted trade and free trade, provided this vital new input. It created a second tier in the management structure with full executive family members as the link between the Boards. It was to be a key development in the future success of the Company.

In 1992 a 'new' Neame joined. The chairman's son Jonathan Neame, a qualified barrister, initially became involved with the Company through his previous career with the Coba Group, a firm of management consultants who had been called in to help formulate a plan for the Company for the joint development, with United Breweries of India, of Kingfisher in the UK. He became a full-time technical director and he also took over as company secretary from Bernard Cork, who had joined as chief accountant in 1972 from Bowaters and was retiring early after 20 years service. Jonathan was appointed to the main Board in October 1993, becoming the first great-great-grandchild of Percy Neame to join the Board and so establishing family continuity to the fifth generation.

Still acquiring assets The early 1970s had proved a significant turning point for Shepherd Neame, and heralded 25 years of expansion. Having begun the decade with pre-tax profits of £148,311, the chairman reported an almost eight-fold increase by 1980, and a 24-fold increase by 1990, despite deepening recession, rampant inflation, strong competition and unfavourable trading conditions in the country and the world at large.

The catalyst had been the purchase in 1972 of 32 Whitbread houses which came available through the government's decision to make major brewers sell off houses in areas where they had substantial representation. By 1973, the first full year of trading results from the purchases, it was clear that these houses had helped create a considerable increase in tied trade volume and were already having a significant impact on Shepherd Neame's profits. It reconfirmed the Board's view of properties as a resource to buy, sell, or re-develop. More importantly, the results confirmed that the Board's postwar policy of expansion was right and it continued to be the way forward: from 1972 to the end of the decade, the Company acquired a total of 65 houses, a significant leap forward.

An extensive programme of improvements to the estate was also carried out in the 1970s and refurbishment included better toilet accommodation and catering kitchens, the updating of private quarters and installation of cellars with cooling equipment which generally improved the quality of beer. Yet not everyone welcomed the changes. One licensee, a First World War veteran who had lived in a Medway town property for 46 years, and still ran the pub as his parents had before him, clearly saw no point in them. He lived in spartan fashion, sleeping downstairs on a camp bed and seemed not to mind the lack

The Crown Inn, Sarre. Shepherd Neame opened the first of its Invicta Inns in 1986 to meet the need for reasonably priced accommodation and food in the Southeast.

of an indoor bathroom. Nonetheless, his house was duly refurbished and, a little later, chairman Bobby Neame visited to see how the work had gone.

> I went over the whole house but he was very reluctant to show me upstairs. Despite improving the accommodation, rooms were full of old possessions and, when coming to the refurbished bathroom, I found he had filled the bath with coal and was using it as a coal bunker!

Customers, too, sometimes bemoaned change, particularly when their local pub's facilities came in from the cold. For centuries the trip to the outside Gents had provided a vital, additional benefit unenvisaged by the original architects – the chance to sober up in the cold air before returning to the fray!

Acquisitions continued apace in the 1980s with 46 more houses joining the Shepherd Neame stable. In 1986, Shepherd Neame opened the first three of its Invicta Inns, the White Horse at Boughton, the Woolpack at Chilham and the New Flying Horse at Wye, to meet the perceived demand for middle-priced accommodation and food in the Southeast. The Company was particularly mindful of the easy availability of inexpensive accommodation in small hotels just across the Channel. Pub grub, which Shepherd Neame had developed, became a major attraction over the years, to the point where a number of well-known chefs actually moved out of the restaurant trade and into pub kitchens.

Repairs and improvements also continued in this decade. The accounts for 1988 recorded £3 million expenditure on the estate, including one unexpected item of £191,000 to replace the roofs of seven houses destroyed in the previous October's hurricane. Still more unexpectedly, in clearing the ground for a new building at the famous old smuggling inn, the Walnut Tree at Aldington, a group of skeletons was discovered, causing much in the way of local speculation until they were found to date back to the fourteenth century Black Death.

Colin Neame (left) and Gerald Hadley raise a glass to the award winning Queen Court wine, the first English wine launched by a brewing company and produced from its own vineyards.

Giving up the farm

In 1982, hop production at Queen Court, the Brewery's farm, came to an end in the face of the need for major investment, falling hop prices and infection by verticillium wilt. Sale of much of the land raised some £716,000, considerably more than the farm's profits for the previous two decades, but it was a controversial decision as the sale made it difficult to make a success out of the remainder of the farm. Progressively the Company also withdrew from its innovative enterprises: feeding yeast to pigs, spent grains to cattle and the cultivation of the vineyard. Shepherd Neame had been the first brewing company to produce and launch an English wine from its own vineyards. The wine, named Queen Court after the farm, won a number of awards in the early 1980s. Finally, however, in part due to

the BSE cattle crisis of the 1990s, the Board decided to withdraw from the farm, and the land was leased out. However, Shepherd Neame continued to purchase traditional Golding hops from East Kent to maintain its beer's traditional hoppy flavour.

The Brewery and its products

Cask beers, the Company's mainstay products, had been going into decline nationally since the early 1950s, but Shepherd Neame benefited hugely from the upsurge in the popularity of traditional draught beers largely brought about by the Campaign for Real Ale in the early 1970s. Nevertheless, drinking habits were still changing, and lager sales which accounted for no more than 1 per cent of British pub sales in the early 1950s had, by the early 1980s, grown to 40 per cent of total volume. Another trend was the development of keg bitters.

Major improvements in brewing equipment took place throughout the 1970s, to match the growing volume of business in traditional cask ales and the development of Hürlimann lager, and a sum in excess of £7m was spent on plant and buildings during the 1970s and 1980s.

The 1980 AGM had more than an air of celebration about it. Shareholders were invited to tour the Brewery to see in operation the new plant which had been opened earlier in the year by William Deedes (later Lord Deedes), editor of the *Daily Telegraph*, and they even enjoyed a lunch at the new training centre and social club at 10–11a Court Street. By the next year a 4-pint canning line had been installed and plans were underway to introduce Master Brewer XX and Hürlimann lager in cans in time for the Christmas trade. Further improvements, alterations and replacements continued apace including expanded storage facilities for draught beer.

In the late 1980s the Company took a far-sighted decision – as the bottle washer had reached the end of its useful life – to abandon returnable bottles. This was coupled with the introduction of shrink-wrapped non-returnable bottles on cardboard trays which did away with the need for bulky cases and meant that beer could be transported over far greater distances without the costly problem of returning bottles.

The bottling line was also improved in the early 1990s and the Company introduced its innovative and distinctive 0.5-litre bottle, initially for Bishops Finger, Spitfire Bottle Conditioned, Original Porter and Master Brew. The shape of the bottle had been conceived to compete against nitrogenated widget cans. Shepherd Neame needed a bottle which came close to producing the same effect. The long-necked 0.5-litre bottle, with its satisfying 'glug' when poured, achieved the object successfully. With its clean, modern lines and the feel of a port bottle, it was 'dressed' to look and feel both user friendly and classy. It proved revolutionary and was duly plagiarised, requiring court action to protect it.

The success of the 0.5-litre bottle helped turn around the fortunes of the bottling line, moving it from a three day a week operation to double shifts. It also led the Company into what would prove to be lucrative export markets. By 1995, exports were made regularly to 12 countries, including the USA, Hungary, Norway, Russia, Japan, Australia and New Zealand. In Sweden, Bishops Finger became the biggest-selling British beer.

It was the French market, however, which proved a spectacular and unforeseen success for Shepherd Neame. Annual sales of Bishops Finger in Calais reached the one million bottle mark, largely due to its popularity with UK holidaymakers returning to Britain. One of the few British ales on sale in the cross-Channel port, Bishops Finger had been finding its way into homes throughout the UK, but its fans were unable to buy the brew locally. Almost by coincidence, this prompted Shepherd Neame to widen distribution of the 0.5-litre bottle outside the Southeast, its traditional home market, and sales of Bishops Finger in supermarkets proved that here was a flagship product for countrywide expansion.

This Steinbock was presented to Shepherd Neame by the Hürlimann brewery on 5 October 1988 to mark 20 years of co-operation between the two companies.

The Company's original decision to sell its beers in Calais had come about almost by accident. Back in 1992, Shepherd Neame voiced its frustration to local MEP Chris Jackson about the damage being done by cheap imports brought back in to the UK by day-trippers and the like. 'If you can't beat them, join them,' he said. His advice was taken to heart.

Legislation and duty challenge

On occasion, government dictats had actually worked in Shepherd Neame's favour with spectacular benefits. The acquisition of the original 32 Whitbread houses in the early 1970s and the later opportunity to buy more houses from the larger brewers were both made possible by legislation aimed at reducing the big brewers' hold on the industry. But generally, Whitehall's interest in brewing was seen as uninformed and damaging interference, especially when Budget Day brought around yet another increase in duty.

A story that's been brewing
for 300 years

In 1975, the chairman told shareholders, with obvious irritation: 'Let us hope that some Government will eventually realise that you cannot continue to levy high rates of taxation as at present and impose Government interference through expensive legislation without eventually "killing the goose that lays the golden egg".'

However, the politicians were clearly not listening. Following the Monopolies and Mergers Commission investigation which had led to the Whitbread purchases, the industry came under almost constant scrutiny both from government and the EEC, epitomised in the late 1980s with yet another MMC investigation which would have far-reaching implications, although not quite in the way government had intended.

The report proposed a number of measures intended to promote choice, reduce prices, and put an end to the industry's huge monopolies by limiting the number of pubs which could be owned by one brewery. Its findings proposed that any national brewer could retain 2,000 pubs but would need to divest itself of 50 per cent of any number in excess of this figure. It also introduced the concept of traditional cask-conditioned beers as guest beers in national brewers' houses, and tenants were given greater security under the Landlord

Shepherd Neame introduced this innovative and distinctive 0.5-litre bottle in the early 1990s. Conceived to compete with the nitrogenated widget cans, the bottle was designed with a long neck which, apart from producing the desired 'glug', gave the product a more user-friendly and classy feel.

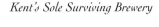

Kent's Sole Surviving Brewery

In 1991 returnable bottles were stopped and the bottle washer was removed from the line and replaced by a fully automated bottle and can depalletizer designed in-house. The bottling line was completely updated in 1996, with the installation of stainless steel bottle and pack conveyors and automatic labellers.

and Tenant Act. Its main findings were hurriedly accepted by Lord Young, the Minister for Trade and Industry, but, in fact, the legislation had exactly the opposite effect to that which was intended. Instead of creating more major players with less market share, the six national brewers accounting for 77 per cent of sales in 1989 were reduced to five with 82 per cent of sales in 1991, a speedy and spectacular justification for those who considered the legislation to be a miscarriage of justice made by people totally divorced from the practicalities of the industry.

Shepherd Neame at that time had 264 pubs, 206 of them tenanted, and was not directly affected by the tied limit. The Company feared that many small pubs and clubs could be forced to close, that jobs throughout the brewing industry would be under threat, and that Shepherd Neame's distinctive ales and lagers could be swamped by a tide of massively advertised national brands. The long-term view was that the consumer could face fewer pubs selling fewer beers at a vastly increased price.

On 1 July 1967 Robert Harry Beale Neame (Bobby), Jasper Neame's eldest son, was appointed marketing director 'with the special task of improving the Company in the eyes of the public'.

It was the spur for the Company to acquire houses in trading areas where it had previously been poorly represented. From years of regular but not spectacular levels of buying, it embarked on a major round of acquisitions, beginning with 33 houses from Allied in 1990, followed by a further 22 from Bass and Courage the next year. It also acquired on lease, free of tie, 60 more houses from Whitbread, the majority in West Kent and East Sussex where Shepherd Neame historically had poor representation. With their addition, the Company was now supplying more than 300 houses in Kent alone. Later, negotiations to buy the leased Whitbread houses brought the estate up to 366 houses, 300 of them tenancies, and gave Shepherd Neame a dominant position in Kent for the first time.

But even as the Board breathed a collective sigh of relief at the MMC outcome, the chairman was warning of another gathering danger. In 1992 he reported:

Kent's Sole Surviving Brewery

Take-home sales in the South East will be affected by imported beers from France, with the introduction of the single market in 1993, where the duty rate is 1/7th of that in the UK. As a result, beers are being sold in Calais supermarkets at less than half the UK supermarket price for the same product. The abolition of EC border controls is bound to lead to French beers being imported and sold in unfair competition with legitimate UK businesses that have paid UK duty.

In 1998 Shepherd Neame led the brewing industry in the fight against duty increase on beer. Undeterred by an unsuccessful outcome to their Judicial Review – in which they argued that the increase contravened articles 5 and 99 of the Treaty of Rome – on 24 March 1998 they sought, and were granted, leave to appeal. A jubilant Stuart Neame shakes hands with Cherie Booth QC who fronted the successful hearing.

At the heart of the problem was Britain's reliance on indirect taxation and, in particular, the perception that increasing excise duty was an easy option for raising funds. Apart from penalising customers, it created an ever-widening gap between duty levels on both sides of the Channel.

Shepherd Neame had campaigned vigorously to draw attention to the problem of 'booze cruise' imports which flooded Kent as tax-weary Britons bought substantial amounts of beer, wines and spirits at considerably reduced prices.

Although by 1997 the volume of imports accounted nationally for one pint in every 20, the level of imports in Shepherd Neame's home market was one in every three. In his June Budget of that year, the Labour Chancellor reversed the previous policy of duty freeze and penalised UK brewers further by imposing an RPI duty increase on beer. With the support of many others in the industry, Shepherd Neame sought a Judicial Review, on the grounds that the increase contravened Articles 5 and 99 of the Treaty of Rome. The case was heard in the High Court in December 1997. The initial judgement went against Shepherd Neame who later sought leave to appeal, which was granted in a high-profile hearing fronted by Cherie Booth QC, Prime Minister Tony Blair's wife. As a result, Shepherd Neame had successfully forced the issue on to the national agenda and gained the support of the brewing industry.

In 1997, Shepherd Neame won its first Royal Warrant – not for a beer but for Grant's Morella Cherry Brandy.

A time for celebration

Shepherd Neame's 300th anniversary therefore dawned in 1998 with a continuing challenge to the Labour government. And the Company which had spent 300 years brewing Britain's finest beers won its first Royal Warrant late in 1997 – not, in fact, for a beer but for Grant's Morella Cherry Brandy. Grants was a Kent-based company founded in 1774 at Dover, bought and revived by Shepherd Neame in 1988.

Shepherd Neame's ability to survive and mark its 300th anniversary as one of Britain's oldest brewing companies was celebrated by a series of major events. In January a dinner was held for the family and shareholders in the Brewers' Company's Hall. In June and July, special dinners were held for brewery chairmen and their wives in the Henry VIII banqueting hall at Leeds Castle and there were two major dances, each for 400, one for licensees and one for employees, at Mount Ephraim, the home of Mary Dawes, the last surviving granddaughter of Percy Neame. These events were a tribute to the dedication of the family members and employees, some fifth generation, who have dedicated their lives to the continuing success of the Company, and the pub managers, tenants and suppliers, customers and shareholders who have given so much support to the Company throughout its existence.

The Company is continually being built on sound foundations and is determined to celebrate its 400th anniversary in the year 2098.

Kent's Sole Surviving Brewery

His Royal Highness the Prince of Wales visited Shepherd Neame on 16 July 1998 to celebrate the tricentenary.

APPENDIX A

Clubs supplied by Shepherd Neame

1. **Between 1906 or 1907 and 1911 in the rather irregular order in which they are listed in the account book**

Clapton Park
Sheerness Conservative
Sittingbourne Conservative
Deptford Liberal
Epsom
Faversham Artillery
Faversham
Dulwich L & R
Fern Lodge
Hatcham Liberal
Kennington L & R
Penge
Swanley Workmen's
South Norwood L & R
Sydenham L & R
Tilbury Liberal
Victoria
West Norwood Reform
Rock Avenue Workmen's, Gillingham
Faversham Golf (1908, 1909 and 1911 only)
Sheerness Masonic
Herne Bay (1909, 1910, 1911 only)
Shortlands Valley (1909, 1910, 1911 only)
Reformers (location unstated; 1910 and 1911 only)
Woodside Social (1910 and 1911 only)
Tilbury Progressive (1910 and 1911 only)
Tilbury Dock (1910 and 1911 only)

2. **After 1921 (clubs with small purchases omitted)**

Allied Trades and Labour (1922–5 only)
Amalgamated Engineers Institute, Erith (very thirsty)
Amalgamated Society of Engineers, Plumstead
Army Pay and Records Social (from 1928)
Ashford Conservative (from 1923)
Ashford KCC Sport (from 1931)
Ashford Workmen's, Bank Street
Ashford Workmen's Whist Villa (from 1924)
Aveley Workmen's (from 1924)
Badshot Lea Workmen's (from 1927)
Battersea Labour (from 1926)
Beaconsfield, Margate (a little in 1921 and 1922; continuous from 1928)
Beckenham Liberal
Beckenham Workmen's
Bellingham Golf (1921–6)
Belvedere North Conservative
Benfleet Yacht (from 1923)
Bexley Heath Labour
Birchington United Services (from 1924)
Blackheath Liberal
Brasenose (from 1925)
Britannic House (1922–37; mainly spirits)
Broadstairs Comrades (1921–3)
Bromley United Services (from 1922)
Camberwell Police Station Canteen (beer only)

Canterbury (from 1926)
Canterbury Foresters Hall (from 1923)
Canterbury Oddfellows (from 1923)
Canterbury Territorial (from 1923)
Canvey Social (1924–8)
Chatham and District Masonic
Chatham Police Canteen (beer only
 1921–32)
Chatham Writers' Mess
Co-operative Employees
Corringham Social (1924–31)
Crayford Social
Cray Valley Memorial (from 1926)
Cricklewood Constitutional
Dagenham Conservative & Social (from
 1927)
Dagenham Working Men's (from 1927)
Darenth Vale
Dartford Labour (from 1923)
Deal Bowling (from 1927)
Denton & District
Downham British Legion (from 1930)
Eastchurch Club & Institute (from 1928)
Erith Magnet (from 1928)
Erith Labour Union (1921–9)
Essex Yacht (from 1926)
Eynsford Workmen's
Farnborough Ex-Service and Old Boys
 (from 1922)
Farningham Men's
Faversham
Faversham Conservative
Faversham Golf
Faversham Ivy Leaf (1921–9)
Faversham Recreation (from 1930)
Frimley Green Workmen's (from 1925)
Gillingham Conservative
Gillingham Ivy Leaf (1921–33)
Gillingham Liberal (great spirit drinkers)
Gillingham Masonic (from 1923)
Glentworth Club Ltd (1922–31)
Gravesend & District Trade
Gravesend United Services (from 1928)
Grays Comrades (1932–40)
Grays Working Men's
Grays & District Labour Party (from
 1923)

Green Street Green
Greenwich Town Social (from 1923)
Hackney Volunteers Social
Herne Bay
Herne Bay Conservative
Herne Bay Constitutional (from 1923)
Herne Bay Ex-Service (from 1926)
Higham Workmen's (from 1923)
High Brooms Working Men's
Hither Green Railwaymen's (from 1932)
Lathol (from 1929)
Lee Workmen's
Leigh on Sea Constitutional (from 1926)
Lewisham Trades & Labour
Leysdown Bay View Social
Leysdown Ives Social (from 1926)
Lower Gillingham Liberal (from 1926)
Lower Halstow (from 1922)
Maltman's Hill Working Men's (from
 1931)
Manchester Unity, Oddfellows
Margate Oddfellows (from 1928)
Margate British Legion
Margate Social
Margate United Services
Margate Working Men's (from 1924)
Meopham Workmen's (1927–35)
Milton Bowling (from 1922)
Milton Conservative (1921–4 and from
 1934)
Minster Workmen's
New Town Social (from 1926)
Newington Social (from 1922)
North Woolwich and Silvertown
 (1921– 32)
Old Brompton Central Unionist (from
 1924)
Paddock Wood (from 1923)
Penge & District Trades and Labour
 (from 1924)
Plaistow Workmen's (from 1922)
Plumstead & District Workmen's
 (from 1922)
Plumstead Common Conservative
Plumstead Common Working Men's
 (from 1927)
Plumstead Conservative (from 1928)

Plumstead Radical
Plumstead Workmen's Union (1921–33)
Portland Cement Works (from 1928)
St Mark's Social
Sevenoaks British Legion (from 1932)
Sheerness Golf (from 1924)
Sheerness Ivy League
Sheerness Masonic
Shoeburyness British Legion (from 1926)
Shoreham Walnut Tree (1924–31)
Shortlands Valley
Sidcup Workmen's
Sittingbourne Cedars (1924–31)
Sittingbourne Workmen's
Sittingbourne Territorial (from 1927)
Snodland Workmen's
South Battersea Labour (from 1923)
South East Ham (from 1932)
South London Social (1921–8)
Southern Railway Bowling (from 1926)
Stone Street (from 1925)
Strood Conservative (from 1923)
Swale KCC Sports (from 1930)
Swanscombe (from 1928)
Swimming & Dancing (not located) (1931-9)
Sydenham Cricket (1923–7)
Tilbury Dock Police (1921–9; beer only)
Tilmanstone Colliery (1923–5)
Tonbridge Working Men's (from 1932)

Tyrrells Hall
Welcome Workmen's
West Dulwich Golf (1921–30 beer only)
West Kent
West Thurrock
West Thurrock British Legion (from 1932)
Westgate Police Station Canteen (1921–2)
Westgate Tennis (1923–31; 1935–6)
Westgate United Services (from 1923)
Westgate & Birchington Golf (1925–36)
Whitstable Social (from 1928)
Whitstable Territorial
Whitstable Yacht (from 1924)
Wigmore Smallholders (from 1932)
Wigmore Workmen's (1925–9)
Woodside Social
Woolwich Arsenal and Town Social
Woolwich Catholic
Woolwich Fire Station Canteen (1921, 1922 beer only)
Woolwich Labour Institute, Beresford Street (1921–32)
Woolwich Labour Institute, Plumstead Road
Woolwich Radical
Wouldham Workmen's (Grays) Sports (from 1931)
York Club Ltd (from 1926)

APPENDIX B

Schedule of main items of plant and buildings
Installed in the Brewery between 1963 to date

Malt Plant

1977   New Boby malt mill.
1977   6 × 20 ton Aldersley bulk malt silos with associated conveyors.
1995   4 × additional 12-ton silos with associated conveyors.
1998   New bulk malt intake point in main car park with associated conveyors.

Brewhouse

1977   Old tubular heater removed from No. 1 brewing copper and replaced by external Briggs Kalandria heater.
1979   New complete 120 brl No. 2 brewing line comprising:
    – 130 brl Briggs copper/whirlpool with Kalandria heater
    – 40 Qtr Briggs mash tun and mashing machine
    – 40 Qtr grist case
    – 2 × 140 brl Burnett and Rolfe hot liquor tanks/overback
    – Liquor and wort heaters, and IPC plant, etc.
1981   30 ton spent grains silo installed complete with Vetter grains blower, and conveyors.
1981   Old hop back replaced by new 130 brl Briggs whirlpool wort receiver.
1992   Old No. 1 copper replaced by ex-Shipstones Brewery 155 brl Shobwood copper with Kalandria heater. New 155 brl Shobwood whirlpool wort receiver also installed. No. 2 copper/ whirlpool converted to operate as a copper only and run into the 130 brl wort receiver to give increased number of brews per day.
1998   Second 30 ton spent grain silo installed in main car park and existing silo resited alongside.

Tun Room – excluding FVs

1974   Wort cooler resited in Tun Room.
1976   130 brl underback built on site by Stewarts.
1978   5 BPH beer recovery plant.
1979   New extension added to side of Tun Room to house 2 × 240 brl Burnett and Rolfe collection vessels. (These vessels were converted to hot liquor tanks in 1994.)
1980   Further extension to Tun Room to house 3 × 120 brl Alfa Laval and 1 × 80 brl Meura collection vessels.
1982   2 × 15 tonne Briggs bulk sugar tanks with hot water heating, built on site.
1986   New yeast plant installed comprising:
    – various yeast collection tanks
    – bottoms and pitching tanks
    – a Eurotechnik yeast press
    – new 20 BPH beer recovery plant.
1986   Alfa Laval centrifuge installed to clarify beers post FV.
1994   3 new 18 brl yeast tanks added.
1997   2 × new 80 BPH APV wort coolers installed to replace old Alfa Laval ones.

Fermentation

The following cylindro-conical stainless steel fermenting vessels were installed:

1972   2 × 120 brl Meura ale FVs.

1973   3 × 120 brl Meura ale FVs.

1975   New Lager Room built with 8 × 240 brl Meura lager FVs.

1976   1 × 120 brl Meura ale FVs.

1977   Main Tun Room roof replaced at higher level and 2 × 120 brl and 2 × 240 brl Meura ale FVs installed.

1978   4 × 240 brl Meura lager FVs.

1982   4 × 240 brl Meura lager FVs.

1985   New FV building built and 5 × 480 brl Briggs FVs installed.

1987   2 × 480 brl and 1 × 240 brl Briggs FVs.

1989   2 × 40 brl Shern FVs (propagation vessels).

1990   2 × 500 brl Holvreika FV's (ex Whitbread/Fremlins) installed outside.

1992   4 × 440 brl B&R FVs (ex Shipstone's Brewery) installed outside.

1994   4 × 500 brl Meura FVs (ex Whitbread Sheffield) installed outside.

Bottling Plant

1963?   New bottling store built between North Lane and the Creek. 30-ft long piles used to support wall adjoining creek with other walls and floor supported on 4-ft wide dwarf walls, due to poor soil conditions.

1966   New Bottling Hall built alongside new store, again with the wall adjoining the creek, as well as some of the heavier items of plant supported on piles.

1966   New bottling line installed with an output of 14,400 BPH in nips, ½ pints and pints. The main items of plant are:
- Dawson 20 wide soaker hydro washer
- Dawson single head decraters and recraters
- Meyer 40 head filler crowner
- Barry-Wehmiller pasteuriser
- 2 Banks cyclone labellers
- Pantin semi-automatic palletizer.

1971   New 4-pint canning plant (made in-house.).

1978   Meyer filler replaced by new Simonazzi 50 head long tube filler.

1986   Non-returnable bottling introduced by the installation of the following plant:
- semi-automatic new glass depalletizer
- bottle twist rinser
- Certipak bottle sleeving machine
- ID shrinkwrapper and tunnel.

1987   Simonazzi filler replaced by a second-hand fully refurbished 60 head H & K bottle and can filler complete with Ferrum seamer.

1991   Returnable bottling stopped and bottle washer removed from the line. Replaced by a new fully automatic bottle and can depalletizer (designed in-house).
Canning introduced and the following equipment installed:
- Hi-Cone can collator
- Sanchez wrap around packer for boxes and trays
- Iwena shrink wrapper and tunnel.

1996   Bottling line completely updated by installation of:
- all new stainless steel bottle and pack conveyors
- new accumulation tables

– new ABL body, neck and foil labeller
– second-hand completely refurbished Kettner wrap around packer
– new Dan fully automatic palletizer with stretch wrapper.

1997 Following additional plant installed to give an increased line output of up to 20,000 BPH and flexibility to cope with the many frequent changes required of bottles/labels/packs, etc.:
– new single deck pasteurizer installed by Bottling Mechanical Services
– additional second-hand fully refurbished 60 Head H & K bottle filler
– additional ABL body, neck and foil labeller.

Filter Room and Process Plant

1966 New Filter Room built adjoining Bottling Hall and fitted out with double ended Carlson filter and 12 BPH Metafilter.
New cabinet cold rooms constructed to house 3 × 80 brl and 4 × 40 brl Meuracoat lined Bright beer tanks.
1976 New 25 BPH Metafilter installed to replace the Carlson filter.
1979 New automatic power handling and dosing system installed to feed the metafilters.
1985 New Beer chiller installed with 80 BPH capacity.
1987 Alfa Laval centrifuge installed to remove yeast slugs from the FVs at output up to 80 BPH.
1988 High gravity brewing introduced and Canongate beer blending unit installed to control final gravity for bottling and kegging.
New de-oxygenation plant (made in-house) installed to feed new blending system.
1989 3 × 120 brl jacketed Bright beer tanks (ex-DBTs).
1990 New 80/100 BPH Metafilter installed in extended filter room, complete with new PLC control system.
1995 2 × 160 brl Shobwood jacketed Bright beer tanks.

Cask Plant

1970 Old Hopkins Goliath cask washer replaced by a Neubecker machine. Purchased second-hand from Heavitree Brewery.
1975 Old gravity racking machine replaced by a Porter Lancastrian single head counter-pressure racker and a second unit added in 1979. Output 90 kils per hour.
1976 6 × 120 brls draught beer tanks.
1977 6 further 120 brl draught beer tanks (three of these subsequently transferred to the Bottling Hall).
1979 Semi-automatic Polypin racking machine.
1983 Additional cask washer (designed in-house) alongside the Neubecker machine.
1989 2 × 40 brl draught beer tanks.
1994 3-Head Endress and Hauser all stainless steel counterpressure racker purchased second-hand from Germany to replace Porter Lancastrian machines and 4th head added in 1996. Output up to 200 kils per hour.
1996 12-head Neubecker all stainless steel washer purchased second-hand from Germany with output to match new racker installed in place of old Neubecker machine.

Keg Plant

1969   Dawson 2-head semi-automatic keg washer installed to feed existing Burnett & Rolfe 2-head racker.
1971   New 2-head UEC semi-automatic keg washer/racker installed to replace above plant.
1976   New 3-head – 2-lane, UEC keg washer/racker (purchased from UEC stand at Brewex). (Output approximately 90 × 9 gallon kegs per hour.)
1984   New Burnett and Rolfe Centrimatic 5-head – 2-lane all stainless steel washer/racker installed complete with new pasteurizer and new all stainless steel conveyor systems, etc. (Output 130× 9 gallon kegs per hour.)
1980–89 6 × 80 brl keg Bright beer tanks.
1996   Third lane added to keg racker, purchased second-hand from Shipstone's Brewery, which increases output to 185 × 9 gallon kegs per hour.

Joint Services, etc.

Boiler House
1972   2 Dodman boilers converted from coal to heavy oil firing.
1973   Vaporax 3000 lbs/hour flash steam boiler installed to augment main boilers.
1978   Dodman and Vaporax boilers replaced by 2 New Robey 18,000 lbs/hour packaged boilers with new steel chimney.

Refrigeration Plant

1974   Old ammonia compressors and brine system replaced by 2 new HTI 75 HP Aquachill packaged chilling units running on Freon R22 refrigerant and circulating propylene glycol around the plant at –4°C.
1975   Additional 75 HP aquachill.
1987   Additional 100 HP aquachill.
1992   Further 100 HP aquachill unit with separate cooling system installed above Keg Plant to supply the Filter Room and BBS tanks, etc.

Liquor

1975   Duplex base exchange water softener complete with storage tanks to supply all the Brewery's needs for soft water. (Output 6,000 gallons per hour.)
1985   Above softener replaced by larger Houseman unit with output of 7,700 gallons per hour.
1989   Christ twin column demineralisation plant installed complete with 350 brl storage tank for all brewing and breakdown liquor. (Output 120 BPH.)
1992   Additional 300 brl demin storage tank.
1998   Third column added to demin plant.

Electricity

1979   New substation with capacity of 800 KVA installed, complete with main distribution switchroom.
1979   Petbow 250 KVA standby diesel generator installed on Keg Plant roof.

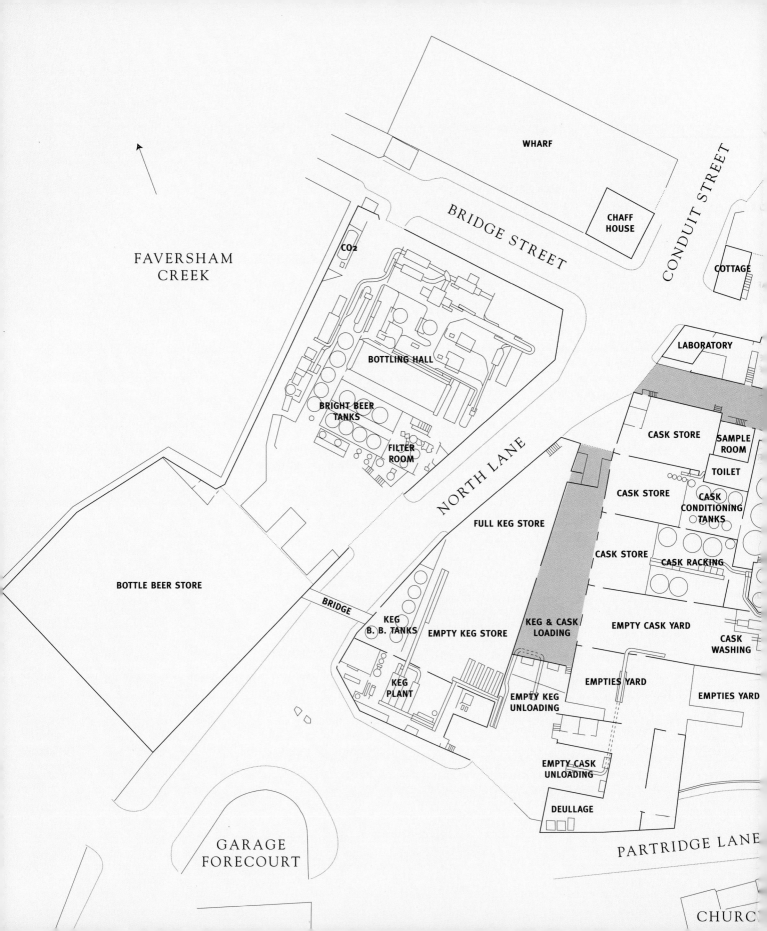

Brewery Plan

Detailed plan showing the layout of the
Brewery as of 1998.

STORE

TWO
BREWERS

STORE

AR PARK

CAR PARK

SPENT
GRAINS

RD

No. 22

WINE & SPIRIT STORE

No. 21

EWERS
FFICE

No. 19

STORE

MALT SILOS

KILN

OFFICES

RMENTERS

BOILER HOUSE

BOARD
ROOM

BREW HOUSE

STORE

OFFICES

FUTURE
FERMENTERS

FUEL OIL

YEAST
PROPAGATION

MATURATION
VESSELS

FERMENTERS

YEAST
PLANT

OFFICES
No. 17

RMENTERS

WORT
COOLING

FERMENTERS

REFRIGERATION
PLANT

HOT LIQUOR
TANKS

OFFICES
Nos. 13–16

SALT

N2

ENGINEERS
WORKSHOP

COURT STREET

HOSPITALITY
No. 10/11a

YARD

ALL

ORIGINAL SOURCES

Shepherd Neame Ltd acknowledge with many thanks their debt to the following sources for background information used in this book.

Duncan Harrison's study of the Faversham Wardmote Books.

The Excise Returns.

Faversham Borough Records.

Peter Tann for his work on the history of Rigdens, based on the Chancery Records at the Public Record Office and the Whitbread archives.

The Shepherd Neame Company Records.

The Commercial Crisis 1847–48 by the City Correspondent of *The Times*.

The Faversham Newspapers and Faversham Annual Directories.

The Economy of Kent 1614–1914, edited by Professor Alan Armstrong and published by Kent County Council, 1995.

The British Brewing Industry 1830–1980 by Gourvish and Wilson, 1994.

Old Faversham by Arthur Percival.

The Shepherd Neame Souvenir Brochure (1948).

The Statistical Handbook, Brewers and Licensed Retailers Association.

A story that's been brewing
for 300 years

INDEX